The Seven Spiritual Weapons

By Catherine of Bologna

Translated, with notes,
by Hugh Feiss, osb and Daniela Re

Introduction
by Hugh Feiss, osb and Marilyn Hall

WIPF & STOCK · Eugene, Oregon

Wipf and Stock Publishers
199 W 8th Ave, Suite 3
Eugene, OR 97401

The Seven Spiritual Weapons
By Catherine of Bologna, and Feiss, Hugh, OSB

ISBN 13: 978-61097-495-0
Publication date 4/25/2011
Previously published by Peregrina Publishing Co., 1998

Text typeface Janson
Titling typeface Trajan

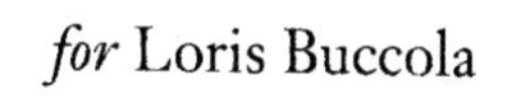
for Loris Buccola

PREFACE

The work which follows is both collaborative and preliminary. The original translation was made by Hugh Feiss, then corrected by Daniela Re, then proofread by Marilyn Hall. Hugh Feiss wrote the first part of the introduction. Marilyn Hall wrote the section on what we believe was Catherine's struggle against depression. All three authors then corrected the proofs. The authors wish to thank Dr. Brian Wyly for his help on the translation and proofreading.

This work is preliminary in the sense that scholars in several countries are working on Catherine's life and writings, and there are sure to be new discoveriės. We hope to be able to produce later editions which will incorporate the result of these ongoing investigations as well as any corrections suggested by readers. Please send corrections to the authors, care of Fr. Hugh Feiss, osb, Ascension Priory, 541 East–100 South, Jerome ID 83338–5655 (email: hughf@magiclink.com).

Our thanks to Bonnie Russel-Lee for the drawing of Catherine of Bologna. Her drawing was inspired by a number of paintings of the saint. Thanks also to Loris Buccola who read the section on Catherine's struggle against depression and offered helpful suggestions. Finally, we are grateful to Margot King for publishing our work in the Peregrina Translation Series.

CONTENTS

Saint Catherine of Bologna
by Bonnie Russell-Lee

INTRODUCTION

St. Catherine of Bologna, much venerated in her own city, has been little known outside of her native region. However, interest in her is now increasing. Scholars are still sifting through archival material and other sources to determine what she wrote and what she painted.[1] Meanwhile, the outline of her life is clear, and her own work, *The Seven Spiritual Weapons*, which is translated below, tells a good deal about her inner experiences and her early years in the cloister. This introduction will situate her life in the history of Ferrara and Bologna. Then, it will study three incidents described in *The Seven Spiritual Weapons* which tell how that external history of the community impinged on Catherine's own experience, causing her great anguish. Finally, the introduction will suggest that Catherine's religious experience was interwoven with her successful struggle against depression.

HISTORY

Catherine's Early Years

St. Catherine of Bologna was born September 8, 1413. At that time, the Holy Roman Emperor was Sigismund of Luxembourg, King of Hungary; three popes contested for the papacy; Giovanni di Michele, the former abbot of S. Procolo, was bishop of Bologna. Catherine's father was Giovanni Vigri; her mother was Benevenuta Mammolini.[2] Catherine had a brother who was a religious and a sister who later joined her in the convent.[3]

Giovanni Vigri was in the employ of Nicholas III of Este (1393–1441), and Catherine went to his court at Ferrara at a young age – how young is disputed by biographers – to serve as a companion for the daughter of the household, Margherita. The Este governed Ferrara as vicars of the pope until 1597. Nicholas maintained the appearances of religion but was promiscuous and brutal in his private life. Catherine seems to have been untouched by the worldly influences at court.

The religious fervour of Ferrara was enflamed several times during the period when Catherine was writing her book. Two Franciscan preachers made their impact on the city. St. Bernardine of Sienna (1380–1444) urged devotion to the name of Jesus; many buildings had the IHS inscribed on them. In her book, *The Seven Spiritual Weapons,* Catherine would write the name "Jesus" 650 times. St. John Capistrano (1386–1456) preached simplicity and virtue. The bishop of the city was then the saintly Gesuate,[4] John Tavelli da Tossignano (1431–1446). In 1438–1442, the beginnings of the Ecumenical Council of Ferrara-Florence were held there.

Her upbringing did not grace her with wide or deep learning, but Catherine had a good mind and learned quickly from those around her. She could read and write Italian, knew some Latin, and was versed in music and the arts.[5] Neither her style nor her vocabulary is of notable literary merit, but her sincerity is transparent as she tries to share with others what she has learned.

Catherine's First Years as a Religious

In 1427, at the age of thirteen, Catherine entered the house of Lucia Mascaroni. This lay community was founded in 1406 by Bernardina Sedazzari († 1425) who wanted to use her dowry to build a monastery for twelve or less professed sisters under the

Rule of Augustine. A papal bull of 1419 authorised the establishment of an Augustinian community, but the bull was not implemented. In 1425, Bernardina made a will in favour of Sr. Lucia. Lucia, who was already part of the community, vowed to carry out Sedazzari's plans. Lucia took up her tasks of leading the small group of women who never numbered more than fifteen. Although the community had neither official rule nor cloister, the sisters were serious and devout. They were guided by the Rule of Augustine since most were tertiaries of the Augustinian Order. They attended Mass at the nearby church of the Holy Spirit which was staffed by Franciscans. When Lucia considered having the community follow St. Clare's Rule of 1253, conflicts arose regarding the direction and status of the community. Lucia was expelled from the oratory of Corpus Domini by Bishop Pietro Boiardi of Ferrara with the connivance of Ailisia de Baldo, one of the community who wished to install the rule of Augustine. In 1426, Ailisia left the community of Corpus Domini and in 1430 was installed by Ludovico Barbo as abbess of an Augustinian monastery. In the end, the Bishop sided with Lucia. To settle the quarreling, he ordered all the sisters to leave the monastery and reside with their families. Catherine left very reluctantly. In a few days, Catherine and five of the sisters who had been there before returned to the monastery. Catherine felt strongly inclined to become a hermit, but she stayed with the fledgling Clarissan community.[6]

Catherine entered the community of Corpus Domini shortly after Ailisia's departure. In *The Seven Spiritual Weapons*, she recognises Mascaroni as the first mother who accepted her into the community. She was answering Jesus' call to serve God with her whole heart. Some external factors may have prompted her decision at that time. Margherita married; Nicholas murdered his wife and natural son in 1425; and her father died in 1426. In her first three years at Corpus Domini, Catherine made rapid progress in the spiritual life.[7]

After three peaceful years in religious life, Catherine had a very difficult period of five years 1430-1434.[8] She felt a strong attraction to the Franciscan spirituality. She selected a Franciscan Observant as confessor in 1429.[9] Several times in her book she praises Bernardine of Sienna, the Franciscan reformer.[10] At this time the Franciscan Order was placed in turmoil by the movement toward "regular observance." The efforts of the observants toward reform were complicated by the simultaneous existence of the claims of three rival popes, each of whom appointed his own Master General and other officials for the Order. The observant movement was represented in the convent of the Holy Spirit in Ferrara where Catherine often attended services.

Verde dei Pio di Carpi, a rich matron and long-time benefactor of the community, wanted to help construct the monastery of Corpus Christi in Ferrara as a house of Poor Clares. She appealed to the Pope. Eugene IV responded by writing the Benedictine Abbot of St. Mary's of Gavello, authorising him to allow Verde to build the monastery and even live there after it was built. He was to appoint the first superior; her successors were to be elected by the sisters. In 1432, Catherine professed the Rule of St. Clare which St. Bernardine and other reformers urged on Franciscan convents of women. The Abbot of Gavello invited some Poor Clares from the reformed convent in Mantua to help form the new community in the Rule in its primitive rigour. The first abbess of the new community was Taddea, sister of Verde dei Pio di Carpi.

Catherine the Writer

In this new community Catherine was the novice mistress. She wrote *The Seven Spiritual Weapons* because she feared that otherwise she would not have fulfilled her calling to form the new sisters of the community. In the book, Catherine is always polite in addressing her most dear and gentle sisters as she invites them to the dance [Preface (5)]. However, she warns them by the very title of her book that the life they have chosen will involve a battle against the world, the flesh and the devil. Their model, teacher and spouse is Christ crucified who obeyed his Father unto death.

Catherine's writings reflect her own experiences and struggles, even though she often speaks of these in the third person. The narrative elements in her work indicate the outline of her own experience as a young religious: after a three-year period of first fervour and joy, she suffered five years of torment, both physical and spiritual. Her prayer became joyless. She suffered from intense headaches, but received temporary relief when she made a general confession. She then experienced three apparitions in which the devil appeared to her disguised as Mary and Jesus. Only then did she achieve peace.

Catherine shares her experiences with her readers, interpreting them in ways that can be understood by relative beginners. Narrative becomes *exemplum*, mystical experience a struggle against temptation, her personal sufferings a model of sharing in the suffering of Christ.

Catherine's book has ten chapters. The preface and first six chapters are a theoretical discussion of various virtues and observances. If the novices will abandon their own desires and choose to serve Christ, they will be worthy of the wedding of the Lamb. Virtue is achieved only by struggle. Catherine discusses six virtues, devoting a brief chapter to each: zeal, mistrust of self, trust in God and a readiness of Spirit inspired by love of God, meditation on the passion of Christ, remembering death, remembering the goods of paradise. The seventh and by far the longest chapter of her work is, she says, devoted to meditation on the words of Scripture. In fact, it concerns discerning between Christ and Satan. Catherine invokes her own experience to teach her lessons. She refers to herself in the third person, but at one point clearly identifies herself with the protagonist of the story.[11]

Chapters 8 to 10 may be said to describe the state of peace which Catherine attained after her first ten years in the community. Both she and the community were at peace. She speaks often of the eucharist, the forgiveness of sins, and, finally, of the Last Judgment.

Occasionally Catherine inserts poetic passages to emphasise certain themes: humility,[12] imitation of Christ,[13] perseverance in one's calling.[14] The passages, often from the *Laude* of Jacopone da Todi, provide a stylistic counterpoint to Catherine's prose and project themes from the restricted scope of her own experience onto a more universal backdrop.

Catherine, the Mature Religious

Catherine was ready to undertake any task, save that of ruling. She regarded herself as the least member of the community, full of imperfections and vices. Nevertheless, as her contemporary Sister Illuminata Bembo[15] testified, her Abbess, Mother Leonarda, sought her advice in chapter and elsewhere. Catherine served as baker for a time, and while she was skilled at her work, the physical effort was too much for her. As novice mistress, she tried to serve her novices and never demanded that they act as servants for her.

Catherine was a very prayerful woman. Prayer aims at union between the soul and God. For prayer to effect this end, Catherine said certain preconditions had to be met: purity of life, proper intention, perseverance, humility of compunction, distrust of self, confidence in God, and a steady awareness of the divine presence.[16] Although Catherine's prayer tended toward mystical union, her intercessory powers were highly regarded. When Margherita d'Este was left a young widow after the death of her saintly husband in 1432, Catherine's prayers saved her from an unwanted second marriage. Catherine's prayers were believed to have defended Bologna from Milanese aggression. In prayer, she beheld the ascent into heaven of the soul of Bishop Giovanni Tavelli when he died in 1446.[17] She herself was discreet and moderate in her own ascetic practices and attempted to live the rule of her convent to the letter.

That convent, Corpus Domini in Ferrara, became an important center for the observant movement among the Poor Clares.[18] A document of 1442 tells us that the number of sisters there had risen to twenty-five and that the abbess was still Taddea Pio da Carpi. In 1450, John of Capistrano visited the monastery where he was received by Abbess Leonarda Ordelaffi and eighty-five sisters.

Catherine, Abbess in Bologna

Catherine was assigned as abbess for the new community of Corpus Domini at Bologna, which was established by her community at Ferrara. The venture was promoted by Third Order Franciscans and by generous benefactions from Taddeo Alberotti. Catherine was forty-three years old when she and fourteen other nuns entered the cloister of the new foundation in 1456. Catherine soon showed herself to be an abbess who cared for the welfare of her sisters and sought to serve them in any way she was able. In 1459, Pius II granted a privilege allowing the sisters of Corpus Domini of Bologna to receive into the cloister Catherine's blind and aged mother, even though she was not a professed religious.

About this time, Catherine herself became gravely ill and suffered from continual hemorrhages. The sisters prayed fervently for a cure. She received the sacrament of anointing. According to Sr. Illuminata, one day Catherine was rapt in ecstasy. She asked for a viola. She began to play it and to sing. God's glory was manifest in her. Catherine seemed to be in the embrace of her heavenly spouse continuously, but she lived on for another year to the joy of her community, which grew rapidly to sixty members.

On Holy Thursday, 1462, Catherine washed the feet of her sisters and then spoke to them of the greatness of the soul and the price which Christ paid to redeem the soul of each. On February 25, 1463, she conducted a chapter of faults, in which she spoke for three hours on prayer. She asked pardon: "My beloved sisters and dear children in Christ Jesus, do not be disturbed by my long discourse, for I hope that it will be the last chapter that I will hold." Catherine died on March 9, 1463. She was buried, but several weeks later her incorrupt body was exhumed. Her body is venerated to this day. She was entered in the Roman Martyrology by Pope Clement VIII and declared a saint by Clement XI in 1712. Her body is conserved intact in the church of the Poor Clares in Bologna.

SPIRITUALITY

Feminine Holiness

Our knowledge of many northern Italian women saints of the later Middle Ages is filtered through the beliefs and convictions of their biographers. Many of these were not convent saints, but married women who achieved sanctity as hermits or in some other non-cloistered context. Their biographers drew on patterns from the lives and sayings of the Desert Fathers to illustrate the sanctity of these late medieval women. They were fierce ascetics, visionaries, leaders in their communities; they fought the devil face-to-face.[19] To be leaders, they had to be public speakers and teachers; and to be teachers, they had to know how to read and write. As such, they transgressed the boundaries of traditional female sanctity and made their biographers nervous.[20]

Catherine of Bologna only partially fits this pattern. For one thing, her life and spirituality are partially available to us in her own words. She did admire and cite examples of the Desert Fathers, but she did not inculcate their fierce asceticism. Catherine did, however, engage in some horrendous struggles against the devil. Her community evolved from a non-cloistered company of devout women to an enclosed convent of Poor Clares. They adopted the observants' interpretation of the Rule. Catherine and her convent communities were esteemed by the magnates of Ferrara and Bologna, but Catherine was never an influential civic figure.

At crucial moments and places, Catherine's life was influenced or even controlled by male ecclesiastics, from her Franciscan confessor during her early years at Corpus Domini in Ferrara to the pope and his delegate, a Benedictine abbot. Catherine did not object to this. She does not seem to have had any ambitions outside living her religious life to the full. This life was cloistered, which limited Catherine's influence outside, but also inhibited the impact of the outside on her and her fellow sisters, giving them space to be and become themselves.[21]

Devils Appearing as Angels of Light

Foletti has suggested that the three appearances of the devil disguised as Mary and Christ which Catherine experienced during the difficult years around 1429–1434 can be understood as referring to conflicts which arose from the evolution of the community. Verde Pio, the matron and benefactress, wanted to help the community become established as a convent of Poor Clares. Her choice was in part guided by the fact that her sister and perhaps a niece were Clarissans at Mantova, an important reform community. However, Lucia Mascaroni was Catherine's first religious superior, and Lucia wished to remain faithful to the founder's hopes that the community would adopt the Rule of Augustine. Lucia's scruple about keeping her oath to Sedazzari was only officially absolved in 1452.

Another conflict concerned which Franciscan observance the new monastery would follow. Verde Pio asked for the observance of Pope Urban, which was less rigid than that of the first rule approved by Innocent IV in 1253. Eugene IV's response did not specify which observance. Oddly, this mitigated observance was not the one followed at Mantua which was to be the source of the Poor Clares who would see to the founding and formation of the community.

When the time came for the first election of an abbess (perhaps after the death of the first abbess who was to be appointed), the community chose Catherine. Very likely she was the candidate of the original nucleus of women to whom the Poor Clares from Mantua had been added. She refused the office. We know that there was some irregularity in the whole process because a pontifical bull of 1434 absolves fourteen sisters of Corpus Domini, including Catherine, of apostasy and interdict and other censures. It seems that in confiding the founding of the community to a Benedictine and stipulating that their confessor was to be a secular priest, Eugene IV had tried in vain to keep the community free of the controversies among the Franciscans. Finally, a papal bull of 1435 put the convent at Ferrara under the observance of Mantua. Thereafter, peaceful growth was possible.

Catherine, however, had been through hell during these troubled years of 1430–34. She speaks of six diabolical apparitions. In three of these, the devil appears as a heavenly being: the Virgin, the Crucified, and Madonna and Child.[22] In the first, the Virgin invites her to exchange her sinful love for a virtuous one. Catherine believes that her sinful love is her tendency to question every order and arrangement given by her superior. In the second instance, the Crucified reproaches her for taking back what she has offered, that is memory, understanding and will, in order to criticise her superior; the third time, the Madonna with Child repeats the first warning about sinful love. The virtuous love the Madonna offers in exchange is blind obedience. It was clear only in retrospect that the devil was speaking in each case, and by God's grace Catherine came to discover that a genuine divine vision is preceded by humility and leaves the soul in peace.[23] Thus she learned that in the particular circumstances in which she found herself, her rebelliousness was a healthy and positive reaction, whereas the admonitions to passive acquiescence were not. These three temptations from the disguised devil occurred between the full remission of sins which Catherine received in 1429[24] and the exit of Lucia Mascaroni from the community and the introduction of

Franciscan observance.[25] Hence, the superior whom she was tempted to disobey was Lucia Mascaroni.

Three other temptations reveal the devil as openly hostile to the community. In the first two, there seem to be echoes of the pressure Verde brought on the community,[26] and in the third a reference to the tensions connected with installing the sisters from Mantua.[27]

Catherine found herself in a dilemma. Verde Pio had the means and the will to introduce the Rule of St. Clare into the community. Such a change coincided with Catherine's deepest wishes, but ran counter to her loyalty to Lucia. In the end she saw that God's will lay with the move to Clarissan observance and that she should acquiesce to what in fact she deeply desired.[28] Nevertheless, she remained loyal to and laudatory of Lucia.[29]

Clearly Catherine's book needs to be interpreted on several levels. She interprets her own mystical experiences as examples which her novices can find helpful in their spiritual and psychological struggles. Those same mystical experiences, as we have just seen, can be read as echoes in Catherine's inner life of the outer events which shaped her community and in which she was deeply involved. Yet, beyond God's grace and the devil's trickery, beyond mystical experience and fidelity to her fellow sisters, beyond and within her common sense and motherly care, there seems to be something else at work, a tension which seems out of place in Catherine's gentle character, a humility bordering on black nothingness. The next section will suggest that this added factor was a struggle against what today would be called depression.

A Struggle against Depression[30]

It has been fashionable for several years now to post-diagnose famous people with depression and other illnesses. Certainly such a diagnosis of St. Catherine of Bologna is possible, but insufficient. That she suffered is evident from her writings; that she triumphed over these sufferings and is acclaimed a saint is equally evident and, perhaps, more to the point in any examination of her depression.

First, to the evidence of her depression. *The Diagnostic and Statistical Manual of Mental Disorders* says, "The essential feature of a major depressive episode is a period of at least two weeks during which there is either depressed mood or the loss of interest or pleasure in all or nearly all activities."[31] The individual must also experience at least four additional symptoms. One item from that list of additional symptoms is "feelings of worthlessness or guilt." In the Preface (1) of *The Seven Spiritual Weapons*, Catherine declares: "I am the least puppy barking . . ." While it is possible to think of this as a metaphor, that the author is deliberately demeaning herself, intentionally becoming one of the 'least of these my brethren' to make a spiritual point, the reality seems to be that she really felt herself to be a puppy, someone not worthy even of the title human, never equal to the refined servants and sisters.

This is corroborated later at IX (9): "My darkened eyes should not have the boldness to praise you . . . my abominable mouth, overflowing with horrible filth . . .;" IX (10): ". . . my nothingness and incomprehensible dejection and mortality cannot praise you, the all-high . . . I am such an unclean and vile worm . . .;" and VII (8): ". . . she seemed to be the most vile and the last of all. She knew that she was unworthy of being among the rest and to see the walls of the monastery. She thought that she was a poisonous plague-bearing snake among her most beloved and venerable mothers and sisters." This may seem overblown to any who have not experienced severe depression, but to those who have been there, it seems a just report.

Again, X (8): ". . . I have no right to expect anything but greatest ruin and confusion before God and human beings." X (9): "The falsity is this, that I have not desired with all my heart, as befits the true servant of our Lord God, that all people hold and recognise me as vile and miserable as I believed and held myself to be, that is, proud, arrogant, presumptuous, evil talking, sensual, a glutton, and like an unclean animal deprived of every ray of reason and a principal cause and agent of every ruin and scandal and lack of good that existed through the whole world in the past, exists in the present and will exist in the future." X (10): ". . . I ought to be held and named the greatest sinner who ever was or can be in the future."

Even in her suffering, however, she is able to imagine some redemption, if not for herself, then for others IX (20): ". . . that if my damnation would add honour to his majesty I might be granted this: that in the bottom of the infernal abyss, if it may be said to have a bottom, he would choose to build with his most severe justice another more horrible and unspeakable abyss where I, as the ultimate and most blameworthy sinner, may be placed as hell's accused upon whom the forge is plied incessantly in order to satisfy the guilt of all the sinners who ever were, who are in the present and who can be in the future."

Other symptoms included in the *DSMIV* list are depressed mood, tearfulness, markedly diminished interest or pleasure in activities. VII (23): ". . . it seems impossible that her eyes would not have dissolved in her head." VII (24): "And her heart could not restrain itself from weeping because of the unspeakable sadness which had wounded it, especially since it was deprived of the flame of divine love by which she was often accustomed to be visited with such abundance that with great effort she could barely hide it. She suffered from great dryness in her head and could not pray nor say the office without great pain and effort. Moreover, in this way, painful sadness increased because she feared that it might be from the vice of sensuality." She was afraid it might have been a vice. She was afraid her depression was her fault, itself a symptom of depression, that one feels oneself to be at fault in everything, especially not being able to overcome depression itself.

Another symptom from the *DSMIV* list is the diminished ability to think or concentrate. VII (25): "As her pain became continually worse, it was as if she were deprived of understanding while the battles raged within and around her." Depression interferes with concentration. Dull pain takes the place of attention. What is possible when not depressed becomes unthinkable during periods of depression.

From the list of symptoms: Psychomotor agitation or retardation and fatigue or loss of energy. VII (29): ". . . she could scarcely hold herself upright . . .;" VII (30): ". . . the malign one . . . received from God the freedom to redouble his rage against her;" VII (32): "Put me in a place where I will have no occasion to see or speak to anyone;" VII (27): ". . . she was deprived of all riches of mental and bodily grace, and the virtues which she had adopted in the beginning with good zeal and without hesitation now seemed impossible for her to have to do. If the virtue of patience were not proposed to her in her mind, she would have very little, but that the slightest word was spoken to her induced in her great bitterness."

When one is depressed, everything hurts, even those words which provide some solace hurt, because they are needed, because one cannot summon up anything on one's own. VII (36): "So he openly permitted that she would know how the above-mentioned apparitions had proceeded from the devil and that God had permitted all that in order to make her come to a great knowledge of herself. And so it happened, because, having passed through the above mentioned hellish punishment which lasted for a space of five years, she was once again consoled by the divine visitation and confirmed in such a great knowledge of her own weakness and nothingness that, if all the blessed souls had sworn to the contrary, she would not have believed it."

One hallmark of chronic depression is the feeling that all of this is happening against one's own better judgment and will. When well-meaning friends and spiritual advisors suggest that one pray more fervently or not take everything so seriously, they are missing the point that a depressed person is being acted upon, has lost all will, can do no more than lie still, and hurt and sleep. Medicine has coined new, medically oriented language for what appears to be a long-standing human condition. Doctors say that there is not enough seratonin in the brain, that brain chemistry is the issue. To Catherine, the explanation was that she was tempted by the devil; it was an issue of warfare even though she could bring to bear on her episodes nothing more than the intention not be done in by them. This intention, held to under desperate circumstances, seems to have been as effective for her as antidepressant medications are for many today.

Whatever the sweet and consequent salvation, no one would ever choose depression. VII (49): ". . . the ditch of mortal sadness . . . 'Which do you want: to return to the aforesaid sadness or to have your head cut off?' Without doubt anyone would respond that she was ready to undergo such a death." Give thanks when it is over and forgotten, maybe, but willingly choose? Those for whom episodes like these are not a choice, but a constant and continuing reality may take great comfort from the writing of Catherine. In instructing future abbesses to consider that there might be some among those in their care who are like Catherine, weak and in need of help before it can be requested, she seems to be requesting what would have made her depressive episodes less horrible.

VII (79): "... whoever wants to go to God through sweetness and consolation is deceived." Here Catherine gives the depressed a great consolation, that the suffering of depression is not endured for naught. Those long periods of dryness, when liturgy seems hopelessly dry and meaningless, like the scratching of a small bug against a huge stone mansion, hoping for entrance, are periods in which the depressed, without any sense of consolation, are called to be faithful to what gives them no pleasure and makes no sense: the holding to a practice that once gave life, a practice that one believes, with no present evidence, will again give life, a practice that at least gives them something to do until the grey fog blanket of despair wafts away.

When the depression lifts, in the subsequent hilarity of life without the gray blanket that surrounded and edged everything, in the sudden vision of a world with gold-edged brilliance, in the sudden peace of a good night's sleep and a morning of no horrible visions or waves of grief, a person is tempted to start 9000 projects. VII (84–85): ". . . astute and mighty devils . . . attempt to command her to begin without discretion to do too much beyond the common rule." Ideas flood the imagination and hundreds of plans are attempted simultaneously. Because something is possible now, everything is possible. The sense of mediation between the extremes of depression and ecstasy requires years to acknowledge and longer to master. Inevitably, everything is not possible, and one is cast, again, into the sinking hole of worthlessness and despair.

By the time she reaches VII (110 ff.), Catherine has learned how to handle her descents into feelings of worthlessness and their (for some) attendant periods of ecstasy. Long hours of being unable to do anything but sleep, the sense of being somewhere else but in her body, of having words come alive are all part of the depressive experience. By VII (11) – "Suddenly there appeared before her the glorious virgin with her most beloved son in her arms" – Catherine is relating a depressive experience, not from within depression but from the period of peacefulness that followed having held the Infant Jesus on the Feast of his Nativity, and that peace enabled her to resist melancholy for a long time VII (118). VII (119) suggests ways to endure: ". . . be prudent and know how to bear patiently the absence of divine love, and in such times, exert yourselves to remain strong in the usual mental and vocal prayer and the other holy virtues and good works until it will please the divine clemency to rekindle the flames of his virginal and chaste love in your heart." To remain faithful in poverty is grand advice for depressed people: when you are unable to think of anything to do or to care about anything or want anything.

Those who experience depression find it very difficult to relate what they have felt and seen to those who have neither personally experienced it nor heard many reports from those who have. VII (122): "It is true that it does not seem thus to those who have not experienced it . . . ."

It seems to be common for depressed persons not to be able to remember one state when in the other. IX (6): "She did not recall the graces, described earlier, that she had received, it was as though they had never happened so much was she beside herself because of the many sadnesses which wounded her heart."

This "little book" reads like a report of three depressive episodes and their resolution with a list of seven weapons to be used against depression. It is written, not in the language of psychology, but of faith and provides a clue for psychology: knowing that these episodes never last forever and holding onto that, in whatever language works, helps people persist and gives them a sense of not being entirely at the mercy of brain chemistry. Additionally, her faith that God will never desert her nor permit anything that could really harm her provides her with interior strength that, however ravaged on occasion, ultimately is her salvation and, by the extension of her sainthood, the salvation of others.

Depressed people live an intensely interior life. This is partly because their exterior lives are lived within the vagaries of their interior lives. VII (34): "She was driven into severe doubt" and "She raised her interior voice . . . ." One day, a greeting from a person has no particular emotional effect, that is, provokes no untoward reaction. Another day, the identical greeting from the same person can completely throw one out of kilter for years, can throw one into great waves of doubt and sadness that incapacitate, frustrate and anger one beyond all sensibility, and the insensibility of it all only provokes one further, because it is not on a sensible level that these reactions occur. They come as if from the devil and not one's own doing. VII (34): " . . . she raised her interior voice, calling out to heaven and asking for divine help."

One can think of the spiritual weapons as weapons not only for the battles of faith, but as weapons for the battles of depression: to intend solicitude and not be misled by the vagaries of mood, to keep steady hold on one's life by not giving in to the swings of feeling, to rest in the love of God, however inexperienced, to hold to the humanity and suffering of Christ as something close and not far away, to remember that death will come in its own sweet time without any need to hurry it along, to avoid the vain pleasures of dissolving troubles in chemicals, to keep passages of Scripture alive in one's heart so they are available in time of need.

What Catherine reveals to chronically depressed people is that the interior voices that rage might be stilled by the interior voices that occasionally console. They might be able to choose interior voices, not always, but occasionally, if they don't let the angry voices go on for too long before attending to them, pretending that they are not there, that they are not hearing, "Wicked, sinful, toad talking, worthless nothing, less than horrible . . . ." as a constant background to their every thought. Equally telling is that she had a confessor; she did not keep her darkness secret but faced the shame of being imperfect and not in control. She gave voice to her darkness, told her fault, thereby weakening its hold on her and making possible the continuation of her daily life which became her salvation, faithfulness in darkness. With divine hope, depressed people can follow the examples of St. Catherine and other holy men and women who have kept themselves faithful in the observances of their monastic lives, rising with their confreres, praying on the days when prayer is impossible and hard, making works of charity a habit of the body if not of the soul and persevering in spite of doubt and suffering, knowing that, whatever the final and scientific explanation of depression, one can honour one's own life and live it out in faith and holiness.

THE SEVEN SPIRITUAL WEAPONS

THE SEVEN SPIRITUAL WEAPONS

PREFACE

CHRIST JESUS

(1) With reverence and sweet and gentle love, I pray that Christ Jesus will guard from the sin of unbelief anyone who comes to know of this little work which I made with the divine help and not attribute to the vice of presumption nor take amiss any error in this present little book. I am the least puppy barking under the table of the honourable and refined servants and sisters of the immaculate lamb Christ Jesus, sister of the monastery of the Body of Christ in Ferrara. I, the above mentioned puppy, wrote this by my own hand only for fear of divine condemnation if I were silent about what could delight others. (2) I also intend that, as the sweet memory of the saints of the past in their books shows, each creature ought to make itself praiseworthy in its creator through the manifestation of the divine Providence conferred upon it by the divine Creator. (3) In this, one will know globally the infinite charity of our Lord God when, through his mercy, he deigns to help and conserve his creation each day, keeping it safe amid accidents and frequent dangers. (4) And, by this, we have an increase of our faith in him, our God the true maker, knowing him to be the conservator of this, his own creation. Thanks be to God. Amen.

(5) In the name of the eternal Father and of his only begotten Son Christ Jesus, of the splendour of the Father's glory, for love of whom, with jubilation of heart, I cry, saying to his most

refined servants and spouses:

Let every lover who loves the Lord
Come to the dance singing of love,
Let her come dancing all afire
Desiring only him who created her
And separated her from the dangerous worldly state
. . .

Placing her in the most noble cloister of holy religion so that, purged there of every stain of sin, she was clothed in the adornment of holy and noble virtue. He reformed the beauty of the soul and leads it back to its first state of innocence so that after this pilgrimage, she can worthily enter into the glorious bridal chamber of her most chaste and virginal spouse Christ Jesus, from whose hand she will receive the prize of triumphant glory. (6) This he imparts to those who, for love of him, abandon the vain pleasures of this weary world, subjecting themselves to the rule of reason and abandoning their self-will, and take refuge in the safe port of holy religion, offering themselves completely to the will of another and following the way of most holy obedience and abandoning their own will in all things.
(7) But, aware that this cannot happen without violence to oneself, I have written here below at some length some counsels to comfort those persons who have entered the noble battle of this obedience and, being strongly attacked and assaulted by their own will and by how they see things or how things appear to them, are very sad, thinking that, by this, they lose all the merit of obedience. (8) That is not true, because every virtue is perfected by its contrary. That this is true I will show later when I will speak of this excellent and beautiful virtue of obedience which is worthily called the queen or noble empress.
(9) So, whoever desires to journey without danger and happily

from this passing life to her heavenly homeland, let her, through the most noble, gentle and kind spouse that she could find and that is, take up this obedience as an impenetrable shield which will give complete victory over our enemies and will be judged at the saving port of eternal retribution, as Christ says: "Whoever follows me does not walk in darkness, but has light."[32] (10) But because at the beginning of this battle and even until its very conclusion, she must pass through a stormy sea, that is, by way of many painful temptations and fierce battles, at the beginning of what follows, I will put some powerful weapons with which to fight legitimately against the cunning of our enemies. (11) But it is necessary that each who wishes to enter into this battle never put down her arms, for her enemies never sleep. So, filled with great fervour and confidence, we take up arms in praise of Christ. Amen. (12) Whoever from deep within her noble and zealous heart wishes to take up the cross through Jesus Christ our saviour who died on the field of battle in order to give us life, let her first take up the arms necessary for such battles and especially those which are treated next in order: first is diligence; second, distrust of self; third, confidence in God; fourth, memory of his passion; fifth, memory of one's own death; sixth, memory of the glory of God; seventh and last, the authority of Holy Scripture as it gives the example of Christ Jesus in the desert.

(13) The soul which is espoused by the priceless ring of good will, that is of divine love, and wishes to serve God in the spirit of truth, must first cleanse her conscience by a pure and complete confession and make a most firm resolution of not wanting ever again to sin mortally, and instead to die a thousand times if that were possible, because the person who is in mortal sin is not a member of Christ but of the devil and is deprived of the goods of holy mother the church and cannot do anything

which will profit her for eternal life. (14) And she does this also because to wish to serve this God faithfully requires a resolution not to sin mortally, as was said above. But note that, should you be in mortal sin, you should never despair of divine goodness nor cease to do whatever good you can do so that in this way,[33] you can get out of sin. And with this hope, always do what is right in whatever state you find yourself.

(15) Besides this, it is fitting that the faithful servant of Christ dispose herself to wish to walk the way of the cross, for it befits all those who serve God to engage in battle against the adversaries of God and to receive from them various painful wounds. And above all, it is necessary to have good and even the best arms, especially those which follow below, to fight against those adversaries vigorously.

I

(1) The first weapon I call zeal, that is solicitude in doing good, since the Holy Scripture condemns those who are negligent and lukewarm in the way of God (Apoc 3.15-16). The office of the Holy Spirit is to inspire in us good inspirations, while our duty is to accept them and put them into operation by waging continual violence against our sensuality which always invites us to what is contrary to that which the spirit wills. (2) Therefore, it is necessary to resist it with true diligence and not to let the time granted to us pass by without acquiring the fruit of good works, as it is written:

> Whoever wishes to go up, let him rest not
> From thoughts, from speaking words and doing deeds
> And always exerting himself in God[34]

but with discretion, so that when our adversary, like a wicked traitor, assails us from ambush, we can defend ourselves. (3) By "from ambush" I mean, when under the appearance of good, he wishes to kill you, for there is as much danger in too much as in too little. And so I tell you "with discretion", aware that this virtue establishes and perfects all the other virtues according to what was said by the glorious teacher of the ancient holy fathers, that is, St. Antonio of Vienna.[35] (4) So it is proper for us to exercise with true discretion all the spiritual and temporal virtues. However, when the enemy sees that he cannot impede the servant of Christ from doing good, he will seek to entice her with doing too much. So exercise all the virtues in proper measure that the weapon of true and diligent discretion may be exercised by us for our salvation and for the praise of Christ. Amen.

II

(1) The second weapon is mistrust of self, that is, to believe firmly and without doubt that one could never do anything good by oneself, as Christ Jesus said: "Without me you can do nothing" (Jo 15.5). Nor could one resist successfully the fury of the infernal enemies for their cunning wickedness. And if someone does confide in her own wisdom and will not do this, let her know for certain that by just judgment she will fall into great ruin and let her be aware that just as this enemy is more malicious than we, so is this wickedness. (2) And therefore, the second weapon for fighting against this enemy tells one not to trust in oneself, and blessed is she who has this noble quality in herself. And to the extent that the person is in a greater state of virtue or exercises the office of prelate, the more she has need for it. (3) I received this example from an old and very proven religious who said that when he was a prelate, whenever he was about to begin some task pertaining to his office of governing the monastery, if he did it according to his inclination, God most often allowed some anxiety or tribulation; and if on the

contrary, he did it according to the counsel and inclination of the majority of his subjects, it always turned out well and often he found himself consoled. (4) Now, then, how could the subject, especially one newly entered into religion, have such presumption that she would want to live by her own lights and her foolish fervour and not rather by the counsel and will of her superior and mistress so that the virtue of holy humility might shine in her and the weapon of self-diffidence might be wielded by her? To the praise of Christ. Amen.

III

(1) The third weapon is to put one's trust in God and for love of him to fiercely wage battle with great readiness of spirit against the devil and against the world and one's own flesh which is given to one in order that it might serve the spirit. And as we stand triumphant with the feet of our affectivity on these enemies, we trust in God with firm hope that he will give us his grace abundantly, by which we will have complete victory over all our enemies and will know that he does not abandon those who hope in him. (2) Whenever the servant and spouse of Christ, by the permission of God, finds herself in a grave and dangerous storm, she cries from her heart toward heaven, saying: "God do not abandon me." Then, however much she feared and doubted whether she was abandoned, she will be raised up by the divine and hidden mystery to the highest perfection with God. (3) We have an example of this in his only Son, when, at the point of a painful and bitter death, he cried out, saying: "Father, why have you abandoned me?" (Mt 27.46). And, therefore, we truly understand how at that point Christ, true Son of God, triumphed in the highest perfection by the accomplishment of obedience to his eternal Father with whom he was perfectly united, so it happened that as man and as eternal

being he said: "My god, my God, why have you abandoned me?" (4) This happened because the divine, united inseparably to him, really abandoned the human and sensitive part in his nature. This was the aim of justice, so that the painful obedience of Christ (Ro 5.19) would cancel the pleasure of the disobedience of our first father. (5) Returning to our theme, the servant of Christ does not fear abandonment whatever it might seem sometimes, for she knows that God our eternal Father will not allow this to happen just as he did not allow it to happen to his own Son. Even then, when she finds herself in great straits and tribulation, she will increase her trust in the divine aid, recalling the sweet promise that he made to us through the mouth of the prophet: "I am with him in tribulation; I will snatch him up and glorify him" (Ps 91.15). (6) Who would not want to be troubled in order to have so sweet and faithful a companion, who offers to be with his faithful in time of adversity? Here we have all the more cause to want to be troubled rather than [to be] consoled, and in this, to hold to firm hope; that is the third weapon we are to employ, entrusting ourselves to God. To the praise of Christ. Amen.

IV

(1) The fourth is the memory of the glorious pilgrimage of that immaculate lamb, Christ Jesus, and especially his most holy death and passion, keeping always before the eyes of our minds the presence of his most chaste and virginal humanity. This is the best means for winning each battle, and without it, we will not achieve victory over our enemies. Every other weapon will achieve little without this one which surpasses all the rest. (2) O most glorious passion and cure for all our wounds. O mother most faithful, who lead your children to the heavenly Father. O true and gentle refuge in all adversities. O supportive nurse who

guide child-like minds to the heights of perfection. O refulgent mirror, who illumine those who look at you and recognise their deformities. O impenetrable shield who most smartly defend those who hide behind you. O manna[36] suffused with every fulsome sweetness, you are the one who guards those who love you from every deadly poison. (3) O ladder most high who raise up to infinite goods those who fly upward upon you. O true and restorative hospice for pilgrim souls. O ever flowing font who provide drink for the thirsty who are inflamed for you. O abundant sea for those who row on you in their derelict boat. O sweet olive tree who stretch your branches through all the universe. O spouse, gentle to the soul which is always in love with you and does not look toward others. (4) And so, exercise yourselves untiringly in this, dearest and kindest sisters, and gaze upon yourselves in his radiant splendour so that, in this way, you can conserve the beauty of your souls. Truly this passion is that wise mistress who will lead you, most beloved novices, to the beauty of all the virtues, and in this way, you will attain the mantle of victory. To the praise of Christ. Amen.

V

(1) The fifth weapon is to remind oneself that we must die. This time is called the time of mercy in which God looks down day after day so that we can amend our lives from good to better. If we do not do this, we will have to render account, not only of the evils we have done, but also of the goods left undone by our negligence. And so Paul the glorious apostle spoke well: "Let us do good while we have time" (Gal 6.10). (2) So often think about death and always stand ready for it, for we know neither the day nor the hour when the most strict judge will command us to render account of the talent of good will granted to us so we could exercise it in praise of him and for the salvation of our soul

and of our neighbours. (3) Novices should especially be on guard, as was said above, lest, out of excessive confidence in themselves, they trespass the rule imposed on them by their superiors and mistresses. They should instead devote all their effort to walking along that way which is marked for them regarding the regimen of body and soul. I say this because sometimes the enemy, with shrewd cunning, leads those who are only slightly instructed in the spiritual battle to think that they must soon die and that they will have little to show for themselves if they do not do further penance. (4) For this reason, the malignant one strives and studies to make them exceed the rule of true obedience which is without any doubt more meritorious than any penance they could do. So it is necessary to use with good judgment this weapon of recollection of our death, so that it can be utilised for the salvation of the soul and for the praise of Christ. Amen.

VI

(1) The sixth weapon is the memory of the goods of paradise which are prepared for those who lawfully struggle by abandoning all the vain pleasures of the present life in accord with the saying of the most holy doctor Saint Augustine that it is impossible to enjoy present goods and future ones too. (2) So, dear sisters, be content not to have in this world any pleasure or any beloved, and do not grow tired of denying your own will, remembering what our patriarch St. Francis said, that is, that the most excellent and greatest gift that God's servant can receive from God in this world is to conquer himself by denying his own will. So he said:

> So great is the good that I behold
> that every wound is beloved by me,[37]

in order to show how, through the memory of eternal things, he rejoiced in suffering evil. (3) And in confirmation of the joys which are prepared for you, dearest sisters, I will offer the following example: when I entered this present monastery, not long after me, there entered a young woman who, after she was here for a little while, tired of doing good and regretted having abandoned the way of the world. And it happened that, being in that frame of mind, she went to make her confession to a very worthy servant of Christ to whom she said that she wanted to return to the world. (4) He was startled by this and responded: "Daughter, be careful what you are about to do for I have received a vision this night or rather early this morning which caused me to wonder a great deal because I did not know what it wished to signify." She said: "Please tell me about it." (5) And he said: "I was led to a beautiful feast where there were countless young ladies all of whom were resplendent with indescribable beauty, and they were clothed with wondrous glory and had garlands of beautiful flowers on their heads. And thus adorned, they walked toward a young lady who evidently wished to walk in their company. And so with much jubilation and festive honour and glory, they drew up close to her to receive her as she wished. (6) And when they were in front of her, she seemed to regret having come and turned around, and when that most noble company saw her do that, it seemed that all Romagna was sad. At that moment the vision disappeared. And then, returning to myself, I pondered what this vision was supposed to signify, but now I understand for sure that God has shown that to me by your coming. (7) For this reason, I beg you, daughter, that you not follow your current evil desire and temptation, but stand strong and persevere until the end, so that you can finally reach that noble feast and company which I saw, and rest eternally with these glorious virgins who await you." (8) When she heard this, she resolved to stay with us, more from shame than anything else. But after a little time had passed, when it was observed that she did not carry herself in a religious way, she was sent back to her family and quickly came to the end of her life amid the vanities of the world. Thus the vision of the servant of God was verified, because, losing the crown of her virginity, she was justly deprived of rising up to the virginal province which the servant of Christ had seen. (9) So, beloved sisters, be strong and constant in persevering in doing good solely for the pure love of our Lord God and hope firmly in the goods of paradise so that you can finally reach them saying together with our seraphic St. Francis: "Those who are just await me until you reward me" (Ps 142.8). To the praise of Christ. Amen.

VII

(1) Of the seventh weapon I will elaborate more at length. I will do this in order to make clear a very subtle trick played on one of the first sisters by the enemy of our salvation. This is the reason that I have been moved to write the present little book as a warning and instruction for all the novice sisters who are here at present or will follow in the future in this monastery, the salvation of whom, together with that of all rational creatures, I have so desired. With the frequent and daily demand of divine help, it seemed to me that in a brief time I would lack the natural powers of my fragile body, so that even with great violence I could scarcely finish compiling this book. The great weakness caused me to tremble, not only in the hand, but also in the head and throughout my body. I would be content, for love of Christ Jesus, if instead, I finished with the mortal path and the deadly deceits of the journey.

(2) The seventh weapon with which we can conquer our enemies is the memory of Holy Scripture which we must carry

in our hearts and from which, as from a most devoted mother, we must take counsel in all the things we have to do. Thus we read of the most prudent and consecrated virgin St. Cecilia where it says: "She always bore the gospel of Christ hidden in her heart."[38] (3) And with this weapon, our saviour Christ Jesus conquered and confounded the devil in the desert saying: "It is written" (Lk 4.1–13). Therefore, dearest sisters, let not the daily readings that you read in the choir and at table go without effect; and let the thoughts which you hear each day in the gospels and epistles at Mass be new letters sent to you by your heavenly spouse. And with great and fervent love put them in your breast, and when you have more time, think about them; do this especially when you are in your cell so that you can better and more securely embrace gently and chastely the things which they command you. (4) By doing this you will find yourselves continuously consoled because you will often receive news from the one whom you love above all else. O how sweet and gentle is the divine discourse of Christ Jesus in the soul of her who is truly enflamed by love of him! Is not the word of Christ's own sweet and mellifluous mouth the evangelical doctrine? Certainly it is, and so how attentively you should listen to it and taste it. (5) And here I put an end to the aforesaid weapons. But in this regard I beg you, dear sisters, that you learn to use them wisely and never be found without them so that you can better obtain the triumph of victory against your adversaries. And be on guard that you are not deceived by the mere appearance of good, for the devil sometimes appears in the appearance of Christ or of the virgin Mary or in the shape of an angel or a saint. Therefore, in every apparition that might occur, take up the weapon of Scripture which shows how the mother of Christ comported herself when the angel Gabriel appeared to her. She said to him: "What is this greeting?" (Lk 1.29). (7) Follow her

example in every appearance and feeling, and you will want to test much better whether it is a good or a wicked spirit before you listen to him. Blessed is whoever does this. Also, it is no less necessary to keep a close guard on thoughts of the mind, since the devil sometimes puts good and holy thoughts in the mind to deceive it under the appearance of virtue, and after that, in order to show what it is, tries and assaults one strongly with the vice which is contrary to this virtue. This the enemy does in order to be able to entice the person into the ditch of desperation.
(8) That the above is true can be shown by what happened in the story about the above mentioned religious who called herself the little puppy. While still young, enlightened by divine grace, she came to the service of God in this monastery and, with healthy conscience and good zeal, was eager day and night for holy prayer, and she strove to make her own every virtue which she had seen or heard to be in others. She did this not out of envy but in order to better please God in whom she had placed all her love. (9) And after some time, when she had received many graces from God and had also undergone great and varied battles and temptations, so much so that one time being assaulted by a mental suggestion and knowing from this that the devil was present to her, she spoke to him very firmly: "Know, malignant one, that you cannot come to me in any way, however disguised, that I do not recognise you." (10) But God, wishing to humble her and show her that the enemy was more malicious and astute than she, permitted one subtle deception, that is, this devil appeared to her in the form of the Virgin Mary and speaking to her said: "If you part from your base love, I will give you the virtuous love." Having said this, he disappeared. (11) Thinking that this had been the Mother of Christ – because at that moment she was then in prayer and was beseeching the Mother of Christ to deign to give her the grace of being able to

love her son ardently – anyway, thinking that the apparition had been the Mother of Christ, when it had disappeared she began to ponder what the Virgin Mary had wished to say when she had told her that if she left her base love, she would give her a virtuous love. And the devil elicited from her mind by a hidden deceit the idea that she wished to say that she should abandon the soul of her own senses and of her own opinion. (12) Because of this, with all her zeal she renewed her effort to obey her superior without any discernment or care for herself as she was used to doing, because in the beginning of her conversion, even before she was obliged to do so, she had loved and desired true and holy obedience more than all the other virtues and to this she had devoted all her zeal. Still, by means of this her enemies sought to deceive her and began to send into her heart various and new thoughts against obedience so that judgments and murmuring entered her mind regarding almost all the things done or said by her superior. (13) And she felt greatest sorrow and bitterness because of this and told her fault[39] to her superior many times and with great shame. And still the battle did not cease. There was much that disturbed her and especially this: every time she received strength not to consent completely, she was violently drawn to it. (14) And then turning herself to the weapon of prayer, she received some comfort. For she did not consent completely but remained in great bitterness thinking that, by this, she was in contempt of the Virgin Mary. She said: "She told me that I ought to leave behind my own opinion, and every day I think the opposite." Thus she was led into great desperation, unaware that this was the result of the devil's instigation and thinking it was purely from herself. (15) When the malign devil saw that nevertheless she did not lose her hope in God, he pondered how to find a more subtle deceit. So, one morning, when she had entered into the church to pray, he suddenly appeared to her in the form of Christ crucified, standing in the form of a cross with his open arms spread somewhat in front of her in a friendly and benign fashion as though wishing to draw her back. He said to her: "Thief, you have robbed me. Give me what you have taken from me." (16) She believed it was Jesus Christ. So with great reverence and fear – as soon as he had appeared to her, she voluntarily had prostrated her body on the ground, so that she appeared to be submissive in mind – she answered by saying: "My Lord, why do you say this to me? For I have nothing; in fact, I am most poor and as nothing in your sight and in this world I am subordinate to others so that I do not have anything." (17) He responded by saying: "I want you to know that you are not so poor and that you have something because I made you in my image and likeness by giving you memory, intellect and will; and by abandoning yourself by a vow of obedience, you have returned them to me and moved me to tell you that this shows you to be a thief." She understood that he said this because of the thoughts of infidelity which she had in her heart against her abbess, as was said above, and she answered: "My Lord, what should I do because I do not have my heart in the control of my free will and I cannot restrain the thoughts which come to me?" (18) He answered saying: "Do as I tell you; catch your will, memory and intellect and make sure that in no matter you do something other than the desire of your elders." And she said: "How must I do this when I cannot retain the intellect which discerns or the memory which remembers?" And he answered: "Place your will in theirs and think that their will is yours and do not wish to exercise memory or intellect in any matter other than theirs." (19) And she even said she could not do that, aware that she did not have her heart subject to her freedom. He said to her: "Do as I told you; that is, sleep, wake and rest." She answered him: "Sir, I do not understand what you want to say." And he said: "By sleeping, I mean that you should not involve yourself in the present things of this world; and by waking, I mean that, nevertheless, you should be zealous about your duty to obey; and by resting, I mean that always and in all your works you keep your mind in continual meditation on my passion." (20) And having said this and many other things to strengthen her in obedience, he disappeared. She, believing he was Jesus Christ, kept her mind on these things and thought about them often. Nevertheless, she did not think she had her heart free from the above-mentioned battle since with great importunity, as soon as her abbess ordered some exercise or said something, it seemed that a thousand judgments came to her mind: "This matter would be better if it were thus and so," and many thoughts of infidelity and contradiction of which she never spoke except in her culpa to her superior mentioned above, as was noted earlier. (21) She did this with great shame and bitterness so that many times she could have washed her feet with the abundance of her painful tears. And she said that if she hadn't made use of this remedy of "saying her culpa,"[40] many times she would have become conceited and rebelled against obeying this abbess, for many times she was tempted very violently to go and fight with her and contradict the things she did or ordered. This could have led to the damnation of her soul, for in no way is a religious permitted to contradict her superiors unless it is a matter of mortal sin. (22) And for this reason when she was thus tempted, she resisted strongly, knowing that it didn't come from herself but from the envy of the enemy, who has the fiercest spite for those people who rightly serve God in the state of obedience, and so he was always searching for new ways by which he could trick her. Hence, she resisted him with patience and will have the crown of martyrdom.

(23) But returning to our plan, when some time had passed, this

battle grew ever greater, and she would never have resisted had she not endured with love and reverence and obeyed her superior in all things. Further, she was never found stubborn or obstinate in her opinions, although by not consenting to the devil she was always involved in a great struggle and in bitterness. So great was the multitude of her tears, which so abounded, that if God had not conserved her sight by his grace, it seems impossible that her eyes would not have dissolved in her head. But when such was her bitter weeping that she reached the point that it seemed no more water could flow, blood came in its place. (24) And her heart could not restrain itself from weeping because of the unspeakable sadness which had wounded it, especially since it was deprived of the flame of divine love by which she was often accustomed to be visited with such abundance that she could with great effort barely hide it. She suffered from great dryness in her head and could not pray nor say the office without great pain and effort. Moreover, in this way, painful sadness increased because she feared that it might be from the vice of sensuality. (25) This fear proceeded from the enemy because, as was said above, already in the first apparition he had said that sensuality arose from him, and now he aroused her, who feared in her heart – not only her, but even acquaintances – that she was sensual. In this way she bore and sustained many rebuffs and accusations. This was the comfort and support brought to her in the midst of so great a plight. As her pain became continually worse, it was as if she were deprived of understanding while the battles raged within and around her. (26) And for this reason, she began to snatch some repose at night and not to stay awake all night as he did, though she was so accustomed to prayer that, even when she was sleeping, she was raised up in the form of a cross, that is, with her arms extended. No doubt this was induced by the enemy so that, by praying too much, she would wear out. (27) And besides this, it seemed to her, and so it was, that what had happened to her was like what had happened to the glorious Job, that is, that she was deprived of all riches of mental and bodily grace, and the virtues which she had adopted in the beginning with good zeal and without hesitation now seemed impossible for her to have to do. If the virtue of patience were not proposed to her in her mind, she would have very little, but that the slightest word was spoken to her induced great bitterness in her. This happened to her after the above mentioned deceits through the great poverty of spirit which she suffered. (28) After some more time had passed in such poverty, since the enemy so far had not thrown her down to the ground, he appeared again. This time he came in the appearance of the Virgin Mary with her little Son in her arms. He addressed her and spoke thus, scolding her: "You have not wished to abandon your wicked self-love, and I will not give you the virtuous love that is my little Son's." And having said this, he disappeared like a person who was upset. And she, thinking that it was the Mother of Christ, pondered very bitterly, believing that she was estranged from her and her Son.

(29) Now let the listener think into what mortal weakness and sadness of heart this led her, so much that she could scarcely hold herself upright, so much that many times she would have despaired if she had not known well that the worst sin that can be is that of despair, and also because the divine goodness never took away the gift of good will, through which she always had the desire of not wanting anything which was contrary to the divine will. (30) And when the malign one saw that through all this he could not obtain her damnation, it seems that he received from God the freedom to redouble his rage against her. Knowing how and how much she loved the honour of this monastery from her heart and the common good of all the

sisters, he sought to afflict her in another way. (31) So, one night, when the other sisters slept, she heard him walking around the monastery like a madman yelling with a frightful and terrible voice. And after this, when he didn't receive from God freedom to destroy the monastery to the ground as happened to blessed Job, he did so much that, in a short while, the monastery was empty of both goods and sisters. But she stood firm and did not wish to go outside until it was promised to her by those who went out of there that she could return and begin again in better surroundings than before. (32) So with this promise, she went outside with great sorrow, saying to those who had come outside: "Put me in a place where I will have no occasion to see or speak to anyone." And thus it was done. After some days, as it pleased divine providence, she returned to that place with five other of those sisters who were there earlier and began to reform the monastery in good order. But a long time passed before they were able to seal themselves in a cloister so that people who came to visit the place went inside. (33) So the enemy made up his mind against her and aroused some people of high status in the world who secretly asked her to please agree to go and stay in their house in the company of one of their lonely little daughters, and said that if it was necessary to obtain permission from the pope or from anyone else, she should not doubt that all which was necessary to the health of the soul and the body would be provided her better than she could know how to ask for it. She did not consent to all these promises, but stayed firmly and constantly in the aforementioned place with full faith that she was still established in the cloister under the Rule of St. Clare. And so it was.

(34) But the enemy, furious once more, began again to want to raze to the ground the foundation of the revealed edifice. She was driven into severe doubt and had recourse to the weapons

of prayer, and with heartfelt affection, she raised her interior voice, calling out to heaven and asking for divine help. And she was fully heard and bore and sustained many and varied tribulations both in her own person and in her neighbours which I am not going to put down here because the list would be too long to tell. (35) But as it is written so it happened: "They called out in the day of their affliction, and you heard them from heaven" (2 Esdr 9.27-28). And so it happened that the building progressed from good to better, and the enemy lost the battle and remained confused. This happened to the praise of the Lord God who does not abandon those who hope in him, who permitted her to have many great troubles because he wished to test her this way and make her worthy of greater glory.

(36) So he openly permitted that she would know how the above mentioned apparitions had proceeded from the devil and that God had permitted all that in order to make her come to a great knowledge of herself. And so it happened, because, having passed through the above mentioned hellish punishment which lasted for a space of five years, she was once again consoled by the divine visitation and confirmed in such a great knowledge of her own weakness and nothingness that, if all the blessed souls had sworn to the contrary, she would not have believed it.

(37) Besides this, she remained in such a salutary fear that before, or rather in the sight of the divine majesty, she saw herself as nothing, incomprehensible and unutterable. And so at some cost, she became rather expert in the diabolical deceits and also in the true and divine visitation about which she says and affirms the following: When God, through his kindness, deigned to visit her mind, suddenly he drew near with this ineffable and trustworthy sign: that is, before him there proceeded the holy aura of humility which, entering her, immediately caused her to incline her interior and exterior

head, so that she appeared to be the principal root of all faults past, present and future. (38) And thus accusing herself of any fault committed in her neighbours, she remained in true and heartfelt love of them. And then, in her presence, shone the radiant sun and true warming fire, Christ, and with this soul he reposed in peace without anything mediating between them so that well could she say: "O high nothingness, your deed is so strong / that it opens all the doors and enters into infinity."[41] (39) And then, as the flame of divine love burned down, the mind stayed illumined, the heart warmed and caught fire with desire to suffer evil, and her face was joyous with jubilant and festive sentiments. And sometimes the eloquence seemed to remain on the ready to augment the virtues and to reprove and to bear with defects gently and sweetly. And sometimes, on the contrary, through the grace of unifying love which abided in her, she remained as though oblivious of any speech. (40) The more she was in tune with God, the more fear she had of being his enemy and of being deprived of him, and in this way, she was able to enjoy the divine presence without danger of vainglory through whatever person he became present. (41) And she also thought that all mortal creatures were equally nothing in the sight of the divine and imperial majesty; in some ineffable way, she was brought an interior light through which she understood that only God could bring her joy and glory and through grace, give her infinite good and through justice, infinite penalty. (42) It seemed to her the summit of stupidity to vainly glory in oneself, and for dread of that to keep from accepting the divine sentiments and from doing good whenever they were revealed to her. I do not say this for the beginning novice but for the perfect who regard vanity as nothing, to which perfection no one arrives with genuine firmness except by carrying the painful cross, passing by way of many temptations.

(43) On the contrary, now wishing to show by its contrary how to understand and recognise the diabolic messengers through the experience which she had in the above mentioned diabolical apparition, she says that in all three occasions when the enemy showed himself to her in the way described, it never occurred to her at that moment to wonder if it was the wicked spirit. Instead, immediately and without any verification, she believed that it was the good spirit because, in these apparitions, the false enemy always preached to her that virtue which she loved the most, that is, obedience. Then with much importunity, he insinuated the opposite, putting in her heart thoughts which inclined her to pass judgment on her superiors. (44) And then, after this, under the appearance of contrition, he aroused so much sorrow over these suggestions that he made her stay in a pit of unspeakable and damnable sorrow, giving her to understand that this proceeded from herself and not from him from whom it doubtlessly did. (45) The enemy kept to this particular method by giving her for a long time the temptation of blasphemy – for which she never found any remedy either in confession or in any other way – until finally the devil came to her one night while she was sleeping and came close to her ears and told her to blaspheme God. She, still sleeping, refused, saying: "I will not do that." And when the evil one saw how much she despised him, he made such a loud racket that she woke up and felt him depart. (46) And in this way, she realised clearly that it was the enemy who had afflicted her so by putting in her heart such blasphemies and then leading her to think that they came from herself in order to make her fall into despair. And after this, she remained victorious over temptation, seeing openly how the enemy insinuated such blasphemies into her spirit. (47) So if any of you, beloved sisters, should be tempted in a similar struggle, do not be alarmed nor saddened by thinking that it proceeds

from yourself rather than only from diabolic envy which cannot stand it that God be adored and praised. But in eternity, without any respite, he will be blessed and praised and magnified and superexalted in despite and derision of Lucifer and all his companions and the dark brigade. Amen. Amen.

(48) Now, wishing to show more clearly what happened to her after the aforesaid deceits, she said that her good will seemed to be partially asleep in relation to doing good, and that the slightest effort began to seem to her like unbearable labour. She was without the taste of devotion to such an extent that everything seemed beyond her, and many years passed before she could recover the taste for prayer. And in the time of these apparitions, she was so strongly tempted by the vice of vainglory that the false enemy placed in her heart that she said that the aforesaid apparitions could be considered good; and by this suggestion he hid himself. (49) Here one should consider with what craftiness the enemy deceived her regarding the way of obedience and then placed in her heart the contrary, and beyond this, caused her to think that these thoughts proceeded from her. And the wicked one did all this to make her fall into the ditch of mortal sadness which was so dangerous that when she was liberated from it, she said that she had feared she would depart. She said: "Which do you want: to return to the aforesaid sadness or to have your head cut off?" Without doubt anyone would respond that she was ready to undergo such a death, even with great pleasure and delight rather than to be returned to this sadness.

(50) Although it may seem presumptuous of me, I sincerely ask all those who will ever find themselves abbesses in this monastery, that they take care to be vigilant over the flock committed to them, knowing that the devil, the hellish wolf, always seeks to devour it. Hence it is necessary to keep a diligent

watch and not wait to save the lamb when it is in the mouth of the wolf or at the point of death, but immediately, with true goodness and generosity, support its weaknesses of soul and body. O how pleasing it is to God and salutary to the subject when the superior gives her help before she asks for it, because what is asked for is less pleasing and less rewarded. (51) And who is so hard-hearted that when they hurt their foot or even their little finger, she does not bend her head to look at it and her hand to medicate it? And while each leader must maintain this manner toward all her subjects without any laziness, the opposite is a deadly medicine, bringing damnation to both the head and the members. Now it is enough to merit this if one does not open her eyes to the dove's simplicity and recommend it to that One who sees all without any rest. (52) She will remember that she must show greater concern for the least soul committed to her than for the whole world with all its decoration. Hers is a very important burden which she should consider well. And always she should show with true prudence greater love for those who are tempted to disobedience and infidelity toward her, rather than toward those who do not follow such a way, because the virtue of obedience is loved more and longingly sought by such a person, as is clear: the enemy always would rather attack the servant of Christ regarding that virtue which he knows is loved by her. (53) That religious is blessed who sustains with patience such barking and conquers herself, because no one will receive the crown of obedience who does not sustain in this way the battle of contradictions, as the infinite goodness of our Lord says; that is, those who conquer themselves will seize hold of heaven.

(54) From this it follows that those who obey with violence to their own opinion and who are vexed in their own will and their own breast and discernment will not lose the merit of true

obedience, but will without doubt acquire a greater share of heavenly glory by doing continual violence to themselves and subjecting their own will not only to their mother and superiors, but also to their equals and those under them. The way of such virtue is manifest in the infinite goodness of the Son of God when he was obedient not only to his eternal Father, but also to his mother and to Joseph as the gospel makes clear when it says: "And he was subject to them" (Lk 2.51). (55) Above all feel ashamed of the pride of the human heart which does not wish to be subject, but always seeks to lord it over others and stand above them. And thus the minds of those persons who are invited to the marriage of the lamb, that is to holy religion, are confounded for they believe that, after a short time during which they stood at the gate of salutary obedience, they are suitable to have the power to rule and manage others. (56) In this they are deceived because, believing they have traversed the way of perfection, they have fallen into the ditch of presumption because they do not consider how far they are from the perfect and humble obedience of Christ Jesus. After the twenty-nine years during which he was subject and obedient, hiding the loftiness of the divinity under the shadow of his virginal humanity, once again more openly and as though he had done nothing by labouring in this obedience, he bore and sustained great and varied sufferings and derision. It is clear that not only was he not regarded as the Son of God he was, but he was even called and regarded as a blasphemer of God and a violator of his law. He was not honoured by the princes and great ones of the world as his servants want to be today, but instead he was considered a fool and an evildoer. He bore and sustained all this in order to be fully obedient to his eternal Father. (57) And he showed that his obedience was perfect when not only was he subject to his Father, but also, through obedience to this Father, he submitted to the lordship of the vilest sinners at whose hands he received so cruel a death; and then he completed his obedience. (58) And because of this example, every person who is called to the state of religion ought not only to desire to stay thirty years or more subject to others as Christ did, but also she should with great fervour ask God every day for the grace of being able to remain in the state of true and humble obedience in order to be more conformed to his Son, who, as was said, not only was subject and obedient to the Father and to human creatures, but to inanimate ones also, because, by taking human, passible flesh, he was subject to suffering from hunger, thirst, cold and heat and other necessities which afflict our weakness. And even through the virtue of obedience, he submitted himself to the cruel mastery of the bitter nails which nailed him finally and decisively.

(59) And how could anyone doubt her salvation if she ended her mortal path in such virtue which makes the servant more like her master than any other virtue? Because of his holy obedience, did not the eternal Father promise Abraham to command his Son to take up our mortality in order to vivify us? Certainly, whoever wishes to build a good building, let her lay down this virtue as her foundation and believe firmly that she will be better saved by this than by any penitence or fasting or contemplation she wishes. (60) There is no rational creature of so little understanding that she does not know that true religion cannot do any greater thing for the Lord God nor anything more pleasing to him than to give her whole self for him, leaving behind her own will, so that it is clear that the creature who subjects herself to others for love of her creator does something greater and merits more than does the one who serves him with her own self-will. And if Abraham was justified for obeying only God, how much more will that one be justified who, for love of God, subjects

herself to obey the servant of this God!
(61) And so, dearly beloved, make firm your resolve, knowing that you cannot do anything greater for your spouse Christ Jesus than persevere and finish under the yoke which you have taken up through him, aware that the enemy sometimes makes the way seem too narrow or too long. And it happens that the novices, suddenly entered upon the field of battle, are placed to the proof so that they are changed from lead into the finest gold, that is, from sensual and worldly, they become spiritual and celestial. And this Our Lord God brings about. He wishes to lead them by the way which his Son walked, who, as we know, from the time of his birth to his death, always walked the way of the cross. (62) And therefore God loves them with a father's love. He wishes to make them co-heirs of the goods of his Son. All of a sudden he begins to place them on the way of the cross, and with his permission they are assaulted by the hellish enemies stealthily, that is, under the appearance of good. In this way he makes them regret so much what they had desired with so much fervour that – since they are in the monastery – the devil puts such terror in their hearts that if it were not for their embarrassment, they would turn back, that is, go outside. (63) This happens especially to those who promise to produce the most fruit on the way of God, for it seems that they have not found God as they had hoped, but also they hesitate to be deprived of him and of every grace and devotion. For first of all they desired his coming with great fervour for the love of God. They undertook to abandon friends and relatives, and the enemy attacked them with the opposite, giving them such recollection and tenderness regarding them that awake or asleep, it did not seem that they could think of anything else but them. (64) And while they were wont to desire to do much penance, they are now attacked by sensuality and greed, so

much so that they hardly dare to take the bread which is placed before them because the devil arouses them so. And for a short while, they are deprived of every taste of devotion so that they enter into great sadness, saying: "Truly I was better off before I came here, and I served God better and with greater devotion than I do now." (65) And so, under the appearance of good, the enemy strives to make them turn back by showing them that the way is too narrow or too long. But in no way should the spouse of Christ consent to such deceits, but with fortitude and readiness of spirit, she should steel her will and say to herself: "If my Lord God permits that I be always tempted to the end of my life, I will never consent, but I will stand firm." (66) And when she has made this resolution, she will go to prayer with as much fervour as she can and say with her heart and her mouth: "My Lord, sweet Jesus Christ, through that infinite and ineffable love which made you stand bound to the cruel torment of the pillar and sustain the fierce and cruel blows of your enemies for my salvation, I pray that you give me such strength that, with the help of your grace, I can achieve victory over my enemies and with patience sustain this and every battle that they can launch against me." (67) And then let her bow about one hundred times more or less, as she is able, at the name of Jesus, invoking him always. Each person who makes such a prayer with a good heart should be certain that she will soon receive remedy and comfort according to the saying and sweet memory of most holy Brother Bernardino whom I call and hold to be the Paul of our patriarch St. Francis, since Christ, wishing to have his life complemented in him, promised one of his brothers to make him as he made the Apostle Paul who could not refrain from pronouncing the name of Jesus. This is precisely what the apostle of Francis, St. Bernardino, has exalted once again in the present not only in his preaching, but also in the devout people which he leads. For this reason he can rightly be called the Paul of Francis. (68) But let us return to our subject. When the aforesaid prayer is finished, if by divine dispensation the temptation has not departed, let the person who has it return immediately without any regard for persons or shame to her spiritual father or mother and mistress and say confidentially: "I say my culpa that I am strongly tempted to depart from this monastery and that I am not happy about this. I pray that you help me, that is that you put me in chains or in prison until this battle has ceased, so that I can persevere in the place to which God has called me." And in this way the one tempted intended that she should be held back when she was drawn to consent.

(69) And the gracious God, seeing the effort that you are making, will command the devil to leave you. He will crown you not only with ineffable glory in the other life, but also in the present life, he will adorn you with many virtues and graces. Of this we have an example of one who, touched by divine grace, left friends and parents and entered a monastery with great fervour. And after a short time he felt such a great tenderness and love for his relatives that he was strongly tempted to return to them, so much so that he seemed drunk with their memory and ran here and there through the monastery as if he wanted to climb over the walls and wept with great sorrow. (70) And seeing this, the brothers had compassion on him and, finding no other remedy that could help him, they thought of putting him in chains. He remained for a while in that penance. As it pleased the Almighty, God promised that the aforesaid temptation would leave him and that he would receive in his soul such graces and adornment of virtue that among the others he was called full of holiness and of divine light.

(71) And in this there lies a demonstration of how pleasing to God is the person who, because of love for him, bears and

sustains patiently all the temptations and adversities which are promised him; hence blessed and more than blessed is that religious, male or female, who is always tempted and never consents, as God said in the Apocalypse: "The one who conquers, I will make a column in my temple" (Apoc 3.12) and so also his glorious apostle St. James says: "Blessed is the man who suffers temptation because when he has been proven, he will receive the crown of life" (cf. Jas 1.2).

(72) Therefore, they are deceived who come to the service of God believing that they will serve him with sweetness and gentleness of spirit and mental peace, because this is not what God gives to his faithful servants; rather, he invites them to battle, saying: "Whoever wishes to come after me, let him deny himself and take up his cross and follow me" (Mt 16.24). We have an example of this in himself, when he descended from heaven to earth not for repose, but to enter into battle and to receive instead of honour, contempt; instead of rest, fatigue; instead of riches, poverty; instead of sufficiency, hunger and thirst; in short, he suffered so many and so serious wounds that he would have wished to die on the field of battle.

(73) And nevertheless, beloved sisters, the bride who has Christ as her groom wishes to be joined to him, agrees to conform herself to him, and submits herself to every bodily and mental torment, but she also intends not to wish to do any specific thing without the permission of her superior, because the virtue of true obedience is worth more than all the others, and it leads those who practice it to heaven. And in any situation, it is safe for the subject person to manifest her temptations which she has received, because the hidden wound cannot be treated or cured. And the more that the situation seems good and safe to her, the more she manifests it, lest under the appearance of good she be deceived as was the one who was discussed above, to whom the

enemy appeared in the form of Christ and of the Virgin Mary. (74) There occurs another deceit which I don't wish to pass over in silence, but will mention to make those who progress on the way of prayer and spiritual savour more astute and prudent. One night, when she was at matins in choir, she felt some kind of consolation in her mind and, believing that the good spirit caused it, she kept saying matins and did not move from choir nor from her place in order not to make a scene. (75) Following the lead of the sentiment which had arisen in her, there occurred a verbal argument in her heart: God had much ennobled man and woman by giving them free will so they could do good and evil, and so when they had done good, God could crown them as if by justice; and the Apostle Paul had said on this point that there was laid up for him the crown of justice because he had exercised his free will in doing good and leaving undone the evils which he had the freedom to commit. After her mind had been occupied for some time in this line of reasoning, she remained thinking that this was the result of divine grace. (76) The next night when she was again in choir saying matins, there came to her such mental exhaustion and such a bodily fatigue that it seemed she could not bear it. With this, the thought struck her that it could be argued that because of the fatigue of the office and the other hardships which she voluntarily bore, she should receive as due her in justice, a higher state than Christ, who had never been able to sin nor to experience any concupiscence enticing him to sin, as had she who had the liberty of sinning and was subject to sin and nevertheless had left the way of vice and sin by exercising herself in virtue.

(77) In this way she suddenly became aware that this was a diabolic message. She had recourse to the weapons of humility, subjecting herself in her imagination to the infernal abyss and considering how she had received from God the gift of good will

without which she could do no good. In this way, she became aware and understood that the consolation she had received the previous night was the work of the devil who wished to lead her to think that she had done good on her own. She was not aware that, because God deigned that we have freedom to do good and evil, we are obligated by debt of justice to do good, and we cannot do it without divine grace. Whoever thinks that he can accomplish something by himself besides fault and defect is really lacking any sort of intellect.

(78) Now, returning to the thread of her argument, with the heartfelt affection of love I ask you, beloved sisters and especially the novices who are here and must succeed in the future, that each put her care to her duty to walk by the way of obedience, because this is the sacrifice which God wishes from you, and for this you must leave every other thing and put this before every prayer and contemplation and mental sweetness.

(79) So blessed are you if you persevere in doing good, neither seeking nor desiring any consolation, for as St. Bernard says: "To serve God is nothing else than to do good and suffer evil, and the rule of the true servant of Christ is never to receive consolation except in time of great necessity."[42] This is the secure way; for whoever wants to go to God through sweetness and consolation is deceived.

(80) So, beloved sisters, do not wish for any consolation from this God, except to finish your life for his love in the state of true obedience and subjection. In this way you will acquire the reign of heaven and in this world you will possess holy prayer and all the other virtues. This is what happened in Blessed Paul the Simple who, in the short time that he served God in pure obedience, acquired the grace of doing miracles.[43] (81) I do not say, however, that a person should wish to walk the way of obedience in order to do miracles, because Christ said: "Learn

from me not to do miracles, but to be humble and meek of heart" (cf. Mt. 11.29). Christ's servants, male or female, neither seek nor desire any miracle except to finish their lives virtuously, persevering in that state to which God has called them. (82) And this will be such a great and wondrous miracle, she will want that it not be known by the ignorance of worldly persons who have no experience of the combat waged by God's servants, male and female, with those enemies, that is, against the deceiving world which always appears to mortal creatures as if it were covered with flowers, and against their own flesh which rebels against the spirit and attacks it constantly with natural weapons, and against the countless infernal enemies who, with much malice and treachery, like wicked traitors, always seek to deceive and kill the souls disposed for divine service. (83) And so such combatants perform a great miracle and provide greater proof beyond any comparison with the soldiers of the world, for there certainly will not be found any man so ignorant that, even if he had wisdom of Solomon and the strength of Samson, he would go into the field of battle and commence the skirmish with his eyes closed, that is, he would not want to fight against enemies whom he could not see.

(84) By this example which I have given, one can rightly comprehend how great a miracle is performed by those servants of Christ, men and women who persevere in good works and so confound the lovers of the world who say that such fighters are mere powder puffs since they fail to consider that they fight incessantly with invisible enemies, that is, with these astute and mighty devils which never cease to assault them in order to draw them back from the way of God. (85) And so great is their wickedness that they also used this other trick. When they see that a religious is fervent and so cannot be drawn back from doing good, they attempt to command her to begin without

discretion to do too much beyond the common rule. And in this way, because she has left the weapon of discretion behind, in a short time she becomes weak or falls into such grave illness that she is constrained to abandon her zeal for prayer and all other virtues. (86) In this way, they are unable to exert themselves on the way of the spirit and become weak and insupportable to themselves, and they deprive God of honour and their companions of good example. And well does it turn out thus, because they had the presumption to have exceeded the counsel of their mothers and mistresses.

(87) Moreover, if the enemy sees that he cannot prevail in this, he uses another tack. When he sees that the religious begins to taste the sweetness of divine love in prayer, he immediately places in her the desire and will to go into a deserted and solitary place, saying: "You know that you would have a better way to taste God, and you could be in prayer day and night as much as you wanted."

(88) Therefore, beloved sisters, be prudent and consider how this counsel and desire does not accord with Christ's true and best counsel which invites you not to follow spiritual sweetness nor the consolations and pleasure of your own will, but to bear the beloved cross, saying "Let him deny himself" (Mt 16.24), which is to say: Whoever wishes to follow me to the highest perfection should sell his own will totally and leave all things and come to the state of religion, which truly can be called the cross because of its continuous denial of self-will.

(89) And that to carry the cross is more excellent than seeking spiritual joy can well be understood through the example of the present generation. Although many men and woman are found in the service of God who experience grand sentiments and visions and spiritual elevations but do not have the grace to do miracles nor to know the secrets of others or to announce future

things as others have, they proceed on the way of the cross in the state of true and humble obedience. (90) One of these was Our Father St. Francis who said that he was perfectly ready to obey and to subject himself to the one who had entered religion most recently. He also said that he would rather have a brother who had passed through the way of temptation and not that of sweetness and consolation, that is, of spiritual sentiments. And he said that the religious must become like a dead man who contradicts no one and, if he is beaten, does not lament but stays where he has been assigned.

(91) Of this we have an example in the most holy virgins St. Marina and Sr. Teodoura[44] and many others who had merited to be holy not for the sake of joys and spiritual sweetness, but because they persevered under obedience not only to their elders, but also to their equals and those younger, bearing with true patience the cross of boredom and fatigue and sweat in their monastery, putting up with cold and heat, hunger and thirst, scorn and shame, mortification and rumour and – in brief – innumerable injuries and persecutions and bitter temptations and battles not only with their own flesh and fragile sex and with furious devils, but also with those from whom they deserved to receive support and refuge in all their suffering and necessity, that is, from their prelates and brothers. (92) And because it was so, how did they hide the meaning of their holiness? They were not those whose names were on others' lips, nor were they regarded as greater, but rather they were the last and the most despised because they hid every grace and virtue that they had, so much so that they were instead thought stupid and sinful, not wise and virtuous. This was not because they put up with mad women, nor because they did some good in the monastery, but because they did not excuse themselves from the blows and bad reputations imposed upon them, but rather thought that the

present misery brought them great happiness.

(93) And truly these are the priceless and beautiful furniture and adornments of the spouses the Emperor, Christ Jesus, our God, who says: "Whoever wishes to follow me, the fountain of life, must go by the straight way" (Lk 13.24). And so that he may comfort your hearts, beloved sisters, know that you are called to the straight way and leave behind vain happiness and natural and corrupt pollutions. Fight manfully with your own weakness and submit your self-will to everyone for the love of God so that, in you, there may be a peaceful spirit which serves as the dwelling place of the Holy Spirit, as he testifies when he says: "Upon whom should my spirit rest, if not upon the humble and meek?"

(94) The beloved companion of our patriarch St. Francis, namely, Brother Giles, teaches what humility we should strive for when he says: "Whoever wishes to possess perfect spiritual peace, which is the true mother of humility and meekness, regards everyone as superior to him; let him love without desiring to be loved; and let him serve without desiring to be served."[45] By such examples you can comprehend well by what virtues you should be adorned as you persevere in the place to which God has called you. And it is well said:

O sinner, will you never repent;
What I redeemed for you by my blood,
Upon the cross with mortal torments?
Sooner or later, I want you to be content.

(95) In order to show that this is the way things are, I do not wish to pass over in silence another thing that happened to the above mentioned religious. The enemy appeared to her in the form of the crucified. At the beginning of her conversion, she entered the present place in which some people were living, and she began to taste the gentle sweetness of the divine love in prayer. For this reason, she conceived a great desire to go in a solitary

and deserted place. She thought she could do much good this way because the place was not yet obligated to the religious life, and so her desire grew very strong. (96) However, she was afraid to trust herself and sought to learn the divine good pleasure. So she began to offer great and almost continual prayer, day and night, asking the divine Majesty to deign to reveal to her what manner of life she should follow. After she had prayed for many days with great care and anxiety, one morning, when she was in the church at this location, about the hour of tierce, she was praying in a heartfelt manner to God that he be pleased to hear. The divine clemency deigned to reveal to her everything she had asked and, among other things which I do not mention now out of proper respect, she was told that a person must remain and stay in that state and place to which God had called her. And then, in order obey the divine revelation, she resolved to stay in this present place, indicating openly that this was what our Lord God willed.

(97) By this sort of event, we can understand that the best thing is to persevere in the place to which God has called us. And be warned that the novice tempted by instability or any other vice not only at the beginning, but even in the middle or near the end, must nevertheless stand firm and persevere, recalling how the holy doctor St. Augustine said that the life of the soul on the earth is temptation, and that blessed is the religious who always struggles and never consents.

(98) And that this is true is shown by this example which I heard from a venerable religious. Once a young man entered a monastery with great fervour in order to serve God. As soon as he had entered and received the habit, he began a great battle against the temptation of wanting to leave. He did not consent although he was made miserable by thinking about it. With patience and constancy, he began to walk the way of obedience

and of the other virtues. With great readiness, he fulfilled all that was imposed on him. Nevertheless, he continued to have that temptation in his heart.

(99) He persevered for a long time in this battle, and he ended his life virtuously in that same place that was predicted for him. God promised that he would work miracles at his death to show how this man had merited the crown of sanctity by the continual temptation which he had borne for love of Christ. By this, we are able to understand how much God is pleased by the virtue of patience which knows how to bear and sustain the temptation and all other contrary and poisonous things that God permits from whatever direction he wishes.

(100) O beloved sisters, remember what St. Bernard said, that delicate limbs don't gather under a thorn-crowned head.[46] But if you wish to be, not only members of Christ, but also true servants and brides, it is fitting that you run the thorn-filled way, following in his footsteps (101) which in brief are the following:

Instead of proceeding with honour and loftiness,
he came to bear contempt and baseness;
instead of with abundance and riches,
he came with poverty and need;
instead of with pleasure and delight,
he came with pain and disgrace;
and instead of with lordliness and freedom,
with obedience and punishment;
instead of with power and health,
with weakness and infirmity;
and instead of with lofty nobility,
with the ox and the ass as company;
instead of with papal dignity like a great priest,
he had Joseph as a companion;
and instead of with regal servants,
the poor fishermen;

instead of coming with heavenly food,
he turned to go begging;
and instead of his divinity,
he took on our mortality;
and instead of the imperial heights,
the thieves in their baseness.
(102) Rejoice, my sister,
walk this way
of Christ the true messiah,
and on it you will conclude your journey
if you do not wish to be tricked,
because all the company
which has gone to heaven
walked along that way.

(103) Dear sisters, if someone thinks that battles and temptations are necessary to true religion, for her it is supreme happiness to be subjected and dejected, and great riches to be poor and begging, and grand honour to be despised, and the optimal height to be basest and last of all things, and great consolation to be afflicted and tormented, and great health to be weak and needy for Christ, supreme and ineffable knowledge to be reputed foolish on account of Him, and finally to live well and to rejoice in eternity and for him to die and finish bodily life with a great and bitter martyrdom. (104) O dearest sisters, these and similar things are the adornments which will make you most beautiful and pleasing in the sight of our eternal, invisible and immortal God, for love of whom I entreat as much as I can that you bear with true patience every anxiety of the present life. (105) And you, novices, guard yourselves from doing what is usual among those with little minds – that is, the stupid and imperfect religious – who like persons of little spirit seem to be in good stead because they are, in their imagination, well-loved and well-regarded by their superiors and masters, but do not

wish to receive a sharp look from them nor a rebuke, and when they are mortified are upset. Such a state of affairs is completely reprehensible, for the good daughter, when she is struck by a blow of maternal charity, should humbly wish another; and the more the subject is led along the strict road of her superior, the more she should feel compelled to revere and love her. She should recall that most humble lamb, Christ Jesus, who was never wanting in obedience to his father, even though by his doing this he was hated, despised and subjected to many painful blows and torments.

(106) And nevertheless, the good and humble obedient person is not saddened – however much he seems to be hated and afflicted and tormented everywhere he looks – and he does not impute this to a human creature but with true patience and fortitude bears it cheerfully through a special grace granted him by the eternal Father which allows him to undergo this in order to become a participant in the inheritance of his beloved Son who invites us to walk on the straight and narrow path and gives us an example in himself. (107) For this reason, the faithful servant does not wish, but ought not be so ignorant that she rejects for herself what happened to her Lord: that is, crucifixion in spirit and body. And so the Apostle Paul rightly said: "We ought not to glory except in the cross of our Lord Jesus Christ" (Gal 6.14).

(108) Furthermore, do not be slow and afraid to suffer evils and to work at what is good.

> If you do not push yourself with great effort,
> you will not be a true spouse of Christ.
> If, however, you bear suffering for him,
> then you will live in glory with him forever.
> And the more that you abandon yourself for him,
> know that in truth you will find him,

and you will never be abandoned.
Hence, it is well said: "Each of you should give all of yourself to blessed Jesus, and with true humility, offer yourself always to his every wish," knowing that the more perfect the person is, the more he is in tune with the divine will, but when one is in the greatest state of perfection, it is necessary that he remain in great fear.[47]

(109) The religious to whom the enemy appeared in the form of the crucified would make you understand this, and, in spite of the aforesaid deception, I can say without any error and with all truth that the grace of God endowed her with such great grace and depth of virtue and victory over temptation that it would take too long to tell of it. But from among many things, I will tell this one to the praise of Christ and as an example and caution for you, beloved sisters, so that you will be careful to remain in great fear after many graces and never think that you have the know-how or capacity to accomplish any good whatever, if not that God, by his grace, gives you light and intelligence to be able to know the diabolic tricks and the strength to resist them. (110) Consider, as was said above, that this sister was partially and for a certain length of time given into the liberty of the devil alone in order to devise within herself the ability to reject and resist the devil's wickedness and power. Nevertheless, before this happened, she had passed through the levels of perfection and had received knowledge of each of these levels as she passed through them. And after all of these, she was shown how her soul was renewed and restored in its first innocence. (111) And besides this, for a long time she endured a very great struggle with sleep, so much so that day and night she could not root it out of her heart, so that in order to offer some resistance to it for the majority of the time, she stood in the form of a cross and in penance at prayer and the divine office and even at mass. One

morning she was with the others and was standing in the form of a cross for the reason just given above and thinking, as she did so, how much was it possible to resist her weakness, and it did not seem that she received divine help in such debility. She was overcome with such desperation of mind that she would have fainted away if God had not then given her relief.

(112) Hence, as the priest was saying the preface and reached the recitation of the "Holy, Holy," at that point, she heard those words sung in the angelic choir which proceed in the presence of so divine and most excellent a sacrament. That angelic song was of such a sweet and gentle melody that, at the moment she began to hear it, her soul suddenly began to leave her body, but she did not cease to hear the words of the Sanctus, although she was completely abstracted from everything. After this, she maintained such a victory over sleep that for a long time she was not bothered by it and could keep awake without forcing herself whenever she wished.

(113) O, dearest sisters, do not regret the lack of sleep and the other austerities, because through their merits, you will merit to reach eternal rest. I want you to realise that she knew that angelic song which is so sweet that there is no tongue which can express it nor mind that can imagine it. But this I can say, that she had heard that most sweet angelic choir for such a short time that it seemed like the batting of an eye; it was so gentle and sweet that almost as soon as it entered into the range of her ears, she renounced herself perfectly and all created things as though they had never existed, and as was said, her soul began in part to leave her body. And it came to pass that she was at that moment standing on her feet and in the form of a cross among the other sisters, but she made not the slightest noise, and she inclined with such gentle modesty that she seemed to weigh less than a feather, and there was no situation that she could not handle.

(114) Now we come to the story of a more marvelous and greater grace granted to this same person by the divine kindness: that is, for a certain period of time, God wished to try her, so he took away the flame of divine love and deprived her mental sight of the sweet presence of Christ Jesus, by whose appearance she was accustomed many times to be consoled. In this way, she came into such bitterness that, day and night, she remained as though in continual weeping, to such an extent that the time assigned to her for sleeping she regarded as a great refuge in which she could better give herself to her painful tears. (115) A short time passed in such indescribable bitterness, as if every consoling thing were for her a source of increasing sadness instead of joy. The feast of the nativity of our saviour Christ Jesus was approaching, that is, the vigil of Christmas was the next day. She asked permission from the mother abbess to remain that night in the church to keep vigil out of devotion. Having obtained the permission, she entered into the church located in this place with the idea in her heart of saying the Hail Mary one thousand times in honour of the mother of Christ, out of penance. (116) And, after she had said a number of the prayers, she continued until about the fourth hour of the night, at which hour it is believed that the Saviour was born. Suddenly, there appeared before her the glorious virgin with her most beloved son in her arms. He had the same form as other little children do when they are born. And approaching this sister, she graciously and with great kindness placed the baby in her arms.

(117) Through divine grace, she knew that this was the true son of the eternal father, she stretched out her arms and put her face over that of the most sweet baby Christ Jesus and with such gentleness and sweetness that she seemed to be completely devoted to him, as the wax is to the fire. And so sweet was the odour that emanated from the pure flesh of this blessed Jesus,

that tongue could not tell of it nor is the mind subtle enough to imagine it. And when one has said all that one can say about the most beautiful and delicate face of this Son of God, it seems as nothing. And so we will leave that to the consideration of the hearers. (118) But well might a lover say to me: O, O, unfeeling heart, harder than any other created thing, how were you not thrown into the darkness and not completely melted like snow when it sees the sun, since you were tasting and gently embracing the splendour of the Father's glory, especially since this vision was not in madness, nor imaginary, nor even by ecstasy, but open and clear with no fantasy? However, it is true that as she lowered her face over that of the infant, the vision immediately disappeared and she remained in such happiness that for a long time it seemed that her heart and all her members would forever be in jubilation. The heartfelt and bitter sadness which had so afflicted her because of the absence of this same Christ Jesus departed from her in such a way that, for a long time, melancholy could not enter into her heart. (119) Therefore, beloved sisters, be prudent and know how to bear patiently the absence of divine love, and in such times, exert yourselves to remain strong in the usual mental and vocal prayer and the other holy virtues and good works until it pleases the divine clemency to rekindle the flame of his virginal and chaste love in your hearts, so that, when God has tested the soul that remains empty of him for some time and has seen that it remains constant and faithful in such poverty, he cannot withhold his consolation and returns to it inseparably with greater abundance.

(120) However, I sincerely urge each abbess who will succeed to office ever after in this place that she use compassionate and maternal love with great diligence in sustaining the mind and body of each subject whom she knows is afflicted with such bitter suffering, especially since there is no sorrow greater than

that which the soul suffers which thinks and believes that she has lost the grace of God. I say "believes," because to believe is not to know in such a case. The reason is this: the soul which is inexperienced in the perfect divine love thinks she is deprived of it when she finds that she does not enjoy the usual spiritual sweetness and that the presence of the humanity of Christ is withdrawn from her. (121) And for this reason, she is afflicted with such mortal weakness that she cannot understand that she is being tested. And nevertheless in such suffering, God in his hidden mystery is joined to her with a triumphal love in the soul. The proof of this is understood from the presence of sorrow, because the greater the love, the greater the sorrow. Hence, the conclusion is that the soul, which lamented that it does not feel love, possesses love and sorrow together and is aware that one does not feel sorrow regarding what one does not love.

(122) But this is not understood by small minds because they love the gift more than the giver. Hence, it is necessary that God withdraw sensory love from the pilgrim soul and remain with it under the guise of sorrow so that she may ascend with perfect love of him by means of this sorrow, which, I truly say, surpasses every mortal sorrow. It is true that it does not seem thus to those who have not experienced it, and especially worldly women, who think that there is no sorrow greater than that which one suffers from the death of one's children and friends and relatives. This is not true, because after the death and privation of present things, these can hope to have paradise from God. (123) But the servant of God, who has focused all her love on him and received her espousal from him, that is, the ring of good will, through which she abandons not only friends and relatives and all created things, but even herself, when she sees herself and then believes that she is deprived of God himself, whose sweet and gentle love she had tasted in part. The result is a pain

and sorrow all the greater and more incom-prehensible because she knows that she can find no greater joy or height than his divine infinity. (124) The result of it is that the pain of this soul is as incomprehensible as God, whom she fears she has lost. Hence, one can conclude that greater pain and suffering test those who go on the way of divine love more than any others. (125) But it is true that all the servants, male and female, of God do not pass through the way of this kind of sorrow, for there are few in the present who pass through the levels of perfection. The latter are the only ones who experience this sort of sorrow through the experience they have had of it. And truly for this reason one can well say: "Many are called, few are chosen" (Mt 22.14), because the spirit of love has become so cold that many less come on the way of this sorrow, because today their natural strength is so weakened that they spend much less time in spiritual exercises. (126) For this reason it is not easy to find those who ascend to the heights of perfection, considering that the weapons necessary to reach this height are so brought to naught (especially that of suffering evil) that one can comprehend how many men and women come to the service of God and live earnestly so that they taste the honey of primitive fervour; but then, slipping from that and surviving the tempest of those temptations necessary to arrive at this perfection, they suddenly fail and come to nothing.

(127) Pray, then, dearest sisters, stand strong and constant in the time of battle, and should it happen that the body is rendered completely weak, keep the desire of the will to do good things and suffer evil ones, so that what you are not able to complete in act, you can complete in loving desire. To the praise of Christ. Amen.

VIII

(1) What follows now reveals still another excellent grace which God granted to the above mentioned religious, to whom the enemy appeared in the form of the crucified. I will tell of this for the praise of Christ and the increase of our faith.
(2) Again, in all truth I can say that this happened to that sister: namely, for a long time she had a very great temptation to unbelief regarding the sacrament of Christ. She doubted regarding the consecrated host. She was much afflicted by this and found no remedy either in confession or in anything else, so with great anguish and bitter lament she called to God almost continuously. And when the time when she should receive communion approached, the temptation increased, so that she did so with such insensibility that she was completely without any taste of devotion. As one time followed another, and she received communion with such insensibility, the battle increased so much that as though drunk with sorrow, she was drawn toward consent. (3) Kneeling in the church among the other sisters, as she was accustomed to do after communion, her heart was so afflicted, that then she raised herself on her feet and stood up, oblivious of herself and without finding a place to be or rest. But the goodness of almighty God, who ordained the struggle and the suffering, prepared both victory and refuge. Hence, one morning when she was spending time in this present church standing in prayer, God visited her mind and spoke to her intellectually. He gave her clear knowledge that the entire divinity and humanity of him who is our God is truly in the host which the priest consecrates. (4) He went on to show how and in what manner it was possible that under these small appearances of bread were present God and man in their entirety. And in brief, he gave her knowledge of everything that

bothered her regarding faith in this sacrament and put an end to the struggles and doubt that she had undergone and could have undergone in the future, convincing her completely with beautiful and natural examples. (5) And beyond this, he showed her how a person who receives communion without a taste of devotion is not deprived of receiving the grace of this sacrament, although she has a strict conscience, even if her spirit is tempted in faith or about some other contradiction but she does not consent. He showed her also that the merit of the soul who receives communion in the midst of such a battle, bearing with patience the spiritual storms, is greater than is the merit of one who receives communion with much sweetness and gentleness. (6) And also she was shown how and in what manner it was possible that the Son of God, Christ Jesus, was incarnate of the Holy Spirit and born of the Virgin Mary without the loss of her most sacred and pure virginity. And he went on to give her open and demonstrative knowledge and understanding of the highest Trinity and many other notable things which I leave out because of my weak memory and lack of strength. All these things were shown to her that morning. Because of all this, her soul remained so consoled and free of this temptation that it seemed she had never been troubled. (7) And in addition to this, the first time that she received communion, when she had received the sacred host in her mouth, she felt and tasted the sweetness of the most pure flesh of the immaculate lamb, Christ Jesus. And that feeling and taste had such a sweet and pleasing savour and sweetness that she could not describe it or give any comparison for understanding it. But truly she could say: "My heart and my flesh exult in the living God" (Ps 84.3). (8) After this, her soul remained ineffably consoled, and her mind was so strengthened in the holy faith of this sacrament that if all creatures had preached against it, she would not have been moved from her conviction. Hence, the sadness that she had suffered before was turned into joy, so much so that, considering the benefit and consolation that she had received through it, she would not have wanted to have avoided suffering this temptation. And thus the great proclaimer Paul the Apostle said rightly: "If we share in his sufferings, we will share also in his consolations" (2 Cor 1.7). (9) And besides this, there remained in her a great and unfailing desire to receive communion often, so that she felt great pain and sadness when she could not do so. So great was this that one time among several when she was in great and gentle weeping so that from her eyes there seemed to issue two abundant streams of water, at that hour, she truly felt her soul communicate in the goodness of divine providence in some ineffable and incomprehensible manner: to the praise of Christ and the strengthening of those new plants, which are not yet perfectly stable in the knowledge of this ineffable and incomprehensible mystery! This happened because our mortal ignorance is not capable of grasping the divine mysteries. (10) And so, beloved sisters, if any of you should, by divine dispensation, be bothered by this sort of unbelief, you need not fear, provided you don't consent, but may trustingly receive him who, out of his infinite love, deigns to come to you. (11) O incomprehensible and deepest profundity of the humility of Christ which not only bent over to take up our base and fragile mortality, making himself obedient unto death, but also in the present and as long as the world will last makes himself obedient and subject to descend each day and each time the sacred words ordained by him are uttered by the priests! These latter are mortal men and subject to fault, although after having received such an excellent office, they should be completely holy and heavenly. (12) And so, most beloved sisters, be not remiss in praying to God for them, that they may be fittingly holy in all their feelings, so that, with divine help, they may more worthily fulfill what pertains to such an unfathomable sacrament and handle in a holy manner the body of Christ, the spotless lamb and your most gentle spouse and the spouse of all chaste and virginal souls. (13) So, then, dearly beloved, let not the way of humble obedience seem narrow to you, but behold, not only on the road, but even in your homeland, the true master, Christ Jesus, our God, gives unceasing example, obliging himself to descend at the act of consecration. And in what manner? Certainly under the appearances of bread, in order to give himself as found to the soul who is still a pilgrim. (14) And therefore:

> O gentle soul,
> do not make yourself so vile
> that he will not take you
> who wishes to come to you
> bestowing his goodness
> to be so kind
> that he does not make
> the wide expanse of his deity
> appear to you openly.
> Now run, sinners,
> and linger no longer,
> for he has become food
> so that you will take him.
> Never is the human heart
> so full of error
> as when it wishes to keep its distance
> from such food.

(15) And therefore, my most beloved sisters, take good care lest the enemy, under the appearance of humility, strive to deprive your souls of the great merit which comes from receiving communion, provided one can do so properly.

(16) And besides this, beloved, remember me, and I pray and implore you as forcefully as I can that not only you, but also those who succeed after you, in accord with the name of the place in which you are called, choose always with all your power to persevere and expand in the sight of God by the observance of a holy life, and in the sight of the Christian people by perseverance in good example, keeping your good reputation not out of self-interest but to the praise and glory of the most sacred body of Christ, to the honour of which that venerable woman, our lady Bernardina, founded and began this monastery, and in memory of the Visitation of her beloved Mother, the Virgin Mary.
(17) Therefore, who would be so bold as to presume to violate the honour and the good name of the church of such a Son and Mother? So, now dearly beloved, with diligent zeal be good guardians and conservators of your holiness "before God and men." To the praise of Christ and the salvation of all his members. Amen.

IX

(1) What follows is also a salutary grace which the divine clemency of our Lord God granted to the aforesaid religious, to whom the enemy appeared disguised as Christ.
(2) Now, because she desired to obtain full remission of all her sins, she began to pray to our Lord, asking him to deign to pardon all her sins, both the guilt and the punishment, and to make this known to her if it pleased him. About the third year of her conversion, it happened that she walked to the church of the Holy Spirit to make her confession to one of those venerable religious men who cultivated the vineyard of our Lord God. Their life is worthy of being praised "before God and men," except that this is truly not recognised by the blind stupidity of

a mind more earthly than celestial. (3) But alas, alas, without doubt not much time will pass before those who accused them, who because of their envy call them "twisted tops," will find themselves so severely condemned by the divine judgment that it will be better for them to have bitten their tongues into more pieces than there are grains of sand at the sea, if that were possible. (4) But returning to our subject, when this person had asked in the aforesaid church may times that the divine clemency deign to hear her, Our Lord God plainly revealed to her that he had pardoned all her sins, both guilt and penalty.

(5) Now, beloved sisters, I have written these things principally for all my dear novices who are newly entered onto the field of the spiritual battle and for those who must succeed them in the future so that they may have grounds for standing always in fear, never trusting in themselves, that is, in their own heart, and they will consider what great graces the above mentioned religious has received from God. Nevertheless, God promised, after all the aforementioned graces, that this religious would be very troubled and deceived by the enemy appearing to her in the form of Christ and the Virgin Mary. And why was this? Solely to rejoice in herself over the power to know and conquer the diabolical tricks and temptations. (6) And therefore it was necessary that God let her be tricked by these enemies for a little while, so that then, humbled, she would be careful to stand in perfect fear and know that God alone can give understanding and strength against his enemies. And certainly that is what happened since she was brought so low and afflicted at the time of the above deception that, not only did she seem to be neither the friend of God nor his servant, but God even seemed to have abandoned her. She did not recall the graces, described earlier, that she had received from Him; it was as though they had never happened, so much was she beside herself because of the many

sadnesses which wounded her heart.
(7) But now, having passed the stormy sea and by the divine grace entered into the land of promise, she sings together with the psalmist the words: "I was brought low and he freed me" (Ps 16.6). She is aware that after this, there remains profound peace and victory in every battle. Hence, she may live without any sadness with the firm hope of her salvation. She awaited with the deepest longing the end of this pilgrimage in order to be joined completely to Christ Jesus, our Saviour. And she had such firm hope in him that, though she was yet in her mortal body, she already seemed to be a citizen of that heavenly court.
(8) To be sure, this did not happen because she relied upon herself, for, although she was in the monastery before any of the others who have lived there during this time, nevertheless she seemed to be the most vile and the last of all. She knew that she was unworthy of being among the rest and to see the walls of the monastery. She thought that she was a poisonous and plague-bearing snake among her most beloved and venerable mothers and sisters.
(9) But, seeing that the goodness sustained and supported her in other labours and in so noble and exalted a place, with humble mien she devoutly called to heaven saying: "O infinite kindness of the majesty of God, I am not worthy to dwell in your house, nor even to thank you for so many great benefits which you have granted to me who am so unworthy. My darkened eyes should not have the boldness to praise you, the sun of justice which, with the radiant light, proceeds from your beautiful and loving face, enlightens the heaven and the multitude of those who dwell in it. And my abominable mouth, overflowing with horrible filth, cannot praise you, the most gentle and priceless balsam from which proceed all the other sweet-smelling and most gentle odours. (10) In short, my nothingness and

incomprehensible dejection and mortality cannot praise you, the all-high and divine God and living and true man, incomprehensible and immortal. But let your highest and most devout charity, which deigns to bear and sustain me and other sinners, be the praise and glory of yourself. And also let your patience, which not only promises that the earth will sustain me, but also that I may stand in your house, even though I am such an unclean and vile worm, be praise and glory to you, infinite good."

(11) And so in all things, she kept to this manner of thanking the divine providence so that, except as was said above, she appeared to be a citizen in the celestial court, she never presumed regarding herself, because God had given her such knowledge of her weakness and nothingness and that of all mortals, that there was no way in which she could glory in herself or in others, but only through confidence in the divine goodness and through the memory of that immaculate lamb who, for her, paid the ransom for that precious burden, that is, his most bitter and hard passion, in the merits of which she had placed all her hope.

(12) And she left this as an inheritance to all her venerable and beloved mothers and sisters in Christ Jesus, praying very insistently that they stand strong and constant in the field of battle, persevering until the end and desiring and searching in all things that which will serve as praise and glory of the most high God, because he says that he will scatter the bones of those who seek to please others instead of him.

(13) And I also pray you with the sweetest affection of charity, that you always love the welfare of the shared and holy sisterhood,[48] supporting with gentleness everyone whom God allows to fall into adversity. Always place every hope of yours in him. I present myself as willing to pray to God, if I receive grace in his sight, as I hope to do, for all those who are here at present

or who will follow in the future in doing the will of God, serving him in the spirit of truth in this holy monastery of the divine and virginal Body of Christ, the sweet and gentle food of holy souls. (14) On the other hand, if anyone either within or without, in the present or in the future, will strive to impede the honour of God, damaging the good name of the monastery for any reason or disturbing the peace of mutual love – which in truth has by means of divine grace remained such up to the present that not even once has there been any quarrel or disturbance in the common sisterhood since they were finally enclosed – I am eager to say, if it is permitted to me, that for such a person I will demand the vengeance of divine punishment.

(15) Above all, let each think carefully about doing what pertains to her state, persevering in doing good with patience and fortitude and holy compassion and maternal love regarding the nourishment of the souls and bodies of her companions so that the wrath of divine judgment will not come upon her. (16) I pray, beloved sisters, that you do good and diligently watch, lest the baneful plague of worldly ambition gain a greater hold among you in the future than it had in the past, especially because I am certain that is the strongest incentive for cutting down the sweet olive tree of holy peace. Alas, alas, dearly beloved spouses of Christ, know for certain that the vice of ambition, together with a lack of holy charity, is what brought down the religious of former times. However, each of you loves and strives to always want to be beneath the others, the least and the last in everything, and with true charity to bear and sustain the spiritual and bodily weaknesses of each other. (17) Most of all I pray for those who will be abbesses in this place. I recall what St. Bernard said, namely, that the superior should never place on the subject more weight than she can bear, so that the good will, which God wishes of the soul, always advances the work. Woe

to those pastors or prelates who, with little solicitude and lack of discretion, are the causes of the destruction of the bodies of their subjects. For these God has given them so that in them the soul may attain his grace.
(18) Now, turning to my own business, with reverence I cast myself on the ground in spiritual subjection, asking a million times and as many more times as I can, pardon from all my venerable and reverend mothers and superiors and all the present and future sisters for every presumption and fault that I have committed in this and in all my life as a religious.
(19) The peace and love of our saviour Jesus Christ, the immaculate lamb, who for me was subject to the cruel torment of the beloved cross, be always with you, beloved mothers and sisters in Christ Jesus. To him I pray that you will be pleased to remember me to his infinite love and mercy which never abandon those who hope in him, even though he promises them some times of great and painful tempests in order to make them more worthy in his sight. In this, may they know the depths of the love of our Lord God, to whom let there be praise, glory and honour now and in eternity. Amen.
(20) He, who for his honour has granted me such a great and unfailing desire, knows that many times I have prayed with heartfelt tears and considered choice that he would deign to give me this special grace: that if my damnation would add honour to his majesty I might be granted this: that in the bottom of the infernal abyss, if it may be said to have a bottom, he would choose to build with his most severe justice another more horrible and unspeakable abyss where I, as the ultimate and most blameworthy sinner, may be placed as hell's accused upon whom the forge is plied incessantly in order to satisfy the guilt of all the sinners who ever were, who are in the present, and who can be in the future. (21) To him I offered myself continually

with heartfelt and considered will, thinking that the head of so many members should be gladdened more by this in the same proportion that the multitude of all sinners is greater than me, a single, putrid member. For it is clear that in the kingdom of our God, the number of those who praise him will be multiplied greatly when, to the numerous community of the blessed, will be associated by grace, the multitude of all the sinners. (22) The blasphemy of a single soul is less dishonour to you my God, than that of such a multitude, even though I am certain that your majesty, God most high and incomprehensible, cannot actually be dishonoured. Lord, if I, so unworthy, cannot have this grace – that by my damnation, offerings of countless graces and praises might be multiplied for you, knowing that one cannot add honour to the depths of your deity – nevertheless, loving Lord, give me this grace: that through my damnation all sinners might be saved; (23) for I know that until now, I have considered the salvation of all sinners a greater consolation and an immense joy without any comparison to my own. And so, without any hesitation or rebellion in my mind, I offered myself to the divine justice, praying that it would deign to avenge on me the faults committed by all sinners so that their salvation would not be denied to me because of justice.

(24) But alas, I fear truly that my petitions will be torn up and thrown back in my face, considering how also the talent of love granted to me on the way never could actually be fulfilled. The reason why would be too useless to recount. But I can say this little about the violence that this heartfelt sorrow which I have borne so long has done to me. I saw that this talent is marvelously granted and given through divine grace to many men and women among those who live in the places which are dedicated to the divine cult, and still they do not actually let this talent grow or expand toward their neighbours, but find it

expedient to hide it in the earth of their hearts, and for this reason they suffer and bear many heartfelt and painful sorrows. (25) But whatever be the cause of this, they knew how to pay their debts, aware that superiors, sometimes deceived, offer the highest charity under the name and word of sensuality, placing before their flock what, for their part, they could not consume nor digest.[49] And this is one of the reasons that observance in the cloister collapses. (26) Alas, that the cunning of the devils increases so much at the present time that they have accomplished so much with their superstitious arts and new discoveries – which are not legitimate to one who considers the matter well with a mind illumined and enlightened by true charity – that in the holy companies, they have no more room for what Christ Jesus, who cannot err, left as his testament to his apostles (there is no need that I recall it to minds which are not childish); and so he wished that, when these apostles found themselves together, they would give each other peace as a sign of true charity, so that with this basis, the fire of charity would increase and broaden. So, also, by contrast we see that, not being wisely exercised, it always falls short. Similarly, a material fire to which no wood is added little by little becomes so cold it dies out.

(27) Experience has shown this, for, not only can we not give the peace together, but also the devil has accomplished so much that, under the cloak of virtue, he has dried up the root of all the virtues, insofar as at present, they do not dare look out for one another. For those who listen carefully a few words suffice.

(28) But he who, through the divine dispensation has been made the physician of other infirmities by the love of God, ponders with diligent scrutiny the useless and damnable ruin that follows from the lack of this fraternal charity, that is, the most noble and necessary virtue that can be in the holy community which is to

know how to bear the chattering and varied condition of each other. This is so weakened and annihilated that the least brusque encounter seems to be an insupportable insult. Would that by this upset, one could better understand how and to what extent it is necessary to always arouse in each other the fire of spiritual and practical charity religiously and piously, so that the enemy, who seeks to damp down this necessary fire, may be totally confused and cast to the depths of the infernal abyss. Amen. Thanks be to God.

X

(1) Now, beloved sisters, so that you will take care to stand with great fear in preparation for the future judgment, I do not wish to remain silent about what God wished to show the above mentioned religious about these matters. This happened before the Rule was adopted in this place of the Body of Christ and at the time when our first mother Sister Lucia di Mascaroni lived here. By the divine will, she received me into this place and was the first one who showed me the manner of serving God with pure charity and maternal affection. (2) I always regard myself as obligated to her, and I always recommend her heartily to all of you, mothers and sisters, reminding you truly you are always much obligated to her, not only for the many buildings which she had erected in this place over many years, but also because the foundation of this place was hers, and always during the time of her humble regime, she maintained its good reputation, its holy peace and its honest life. To the praise of Christ, in whose presence I hope that we will finally be found together rejoicing with her. So be it. Amen.

Now, returning to my task, I wish to tell of the vision that I have kept of the final judgment which is what follows next.

(3) Around the year of our Lord Jesus Christ, 1431, while the

afore-mentioned religious was living in the present place, against whom the malign enemy waged the battles described earlier, I say truly with all honesty, that her spirit was drawn to see the manner of the final judgment in this form; that is, she saw the most high God standing in a human form and aspect high in the clouds of heaven, and he was cloaked in red, and he had his face turned toward the west. And a little below, not far away, was our advocate the Virgin Mary. She was clothed and cloaked in white and stood in silence, her gaze raised up and admiring. (4) And beyond her a little way were the most holy apostles who sat upon seats resplendent like the flame of a great fire. Much further down from them was a numberless multitude of men and women. And all stood on their feet and turned their faces toward heaven to look at God. In the middle of them was one who preached with a great voice. And this same religious who saw this was on the right hand of God and stood within those who formed the great multitude, and with a loud voice she cried to God saying with much happiness and joy some words which I will pass over in silence now. (5) And when the vision was finished, she returned to herself, and she cherished and pondered the things which she had seen and began to think what was the meaning of what she had been shown. And, wishing to be certain of this, she prayed, asking the most high God to deign to reveal to her what had been shown her, whether it is was the final judgment or rather was only a diabolical illusion. As a result – "whoever you are who read this understand" (cf. Mark 13.14) – she was truly assured about what she had experienced and the divine vision and what was revealed to her about its meaning and that, soon, what she had seen would be fulfilled, that is, in a short time the final judgment would come to pass. (6) For which reason, dearest and kindest mothers and sisters, I have prayed most insistently that you will never tire of placating the divine justice with your prayer and to suffer evils for Christ so that he will deign to bear and carry the multitude of innumerable faults committed daily by human nature, and especially for the abominable sin which is contrary to the virginal and chaste beauty of Christ and of his most holy mother, and for ambitious pride and cruel greed which now reign in every generation of people. (7) And these are the principal vices because of which the Christian people are in continuous struggle and battle. Now true charity is so beleaguered that even natural love has no more place, so that one finds no peace between father and son and brothers. And these are the infallible signs of the approaching final judgment. But no more about this since it would be too much for us to say.

(8) But now, returning to my heart and considering that in this last judgment, human faults will be revealed to all, I do not wish at present to hide mine but to reveal them, knowing that confessed faults are in part purged and even better pardoned. And therefore, conscious that after the aforesaid things, examining with diligence the vocation given me, I say truly, that because of the falseness that I have found in me, I have no right to expect anything but the greatest ruin and confusion before God and human beings. (9) The falsity is this, that I have not desired with all my heart, as befits the true servant of our Lord God, that all people hold and recognise me as vile and miserable as I believed and held myself to be, that is, proud, arrogant, presumptuous, evil talking, sensual, a glutton, and like an unclean animal deprived of every ray of reason and a principal cause and agent of every ruin and scandal and lack of good that existed through the whole world in the past, exists in the present and will exist in the future. (10) Whence, justly for all these and many other evils and sins which I cannot say, I ought to be held and named the greatest sinner who ever was or can be in the

future.

(11) But, truly, I confess that, in fact thus far, I have known nothing of my vile nothingness, because, if I had known it in truth, I would not have dared to lift my eyes to heaven, or even to the worst place that could be found. Whence, in the murky depths of the infernal abyss, I do not find a place which is suitable for my plague-bearing carrion so that there justice may be fulfilled in tormenting the one who has offended the divine goodness. And so, since no justice is found in me, it follows that outside of me there is no place so abominable and horrible that it suits me, but only myself. And therefore, I will simply remain in me because I am the most murky and fetid place that can be found. (12) But alas, knowledge of such things has been useful to me, since with full heart and anxious desire, I sought and desired supremely that justice would have its place here, so that every intellectual creature would regard and know me to have become as was described above. Whereas I had desired the contrary, that is, honour and power and also a reputation for sanctity, nonetheless, having abused, through negligence, the desire of suffering evil, it follows I have not faithfully kept the priceless talent of good will that our Lord God gave me through his goodness; (13) because I have received from Him this highest gift of being called to his service, it follows that I should exert all my effort with genuine diligence to conform myself to him, that is, to wish to undergo every suffering and to travel the way of the cross, refusing all happiness and consolation, and desiring that I be hated, and honouring gently any person who has despised me, and serving those who have done me disservice, and speaking good things from my heart about those who have said evil things about me. I know that I rightly merited that they should spit in my face rather than show benevolence, and that those who have been of more help to me in this ought

to be more loved and revered by me. For I know that, by such things, I would be more conformed to Christ, my sweet Lord, than in any other way. (14) And seeing the great tepidity that I have exercised in this, I can truly say that I have lived in great falsity, having the name of serving Christ and not loving what He has come to bear with so much ardour of love, that is, the beloved cross.

(15) Alas, what a great error it is that I have taken so long to recognise. Although in the beginning of my conversion, I sometimes took delight in injuries, and from this sometimes I received spiritual consolations, nonetheless, that first fervour receded, and many years passed in great lukewarmness. I did not seek with diligent zeal what was proper to me as I said above, that is, to be injured, mocked, despised and slandered, and subjected to every least and vile creature so that, in this way, I could make a slight recompense for the injury of their creator who was offended countless times for me and by me. (16) Alas, my naked soul is completely deprived of those honourable and royal qualities that belong to it. Tell me, which aspect do you expect to see appear before the beautiful face of the splendour of the Father's glory. That is, the Son of God most high? As you know, it seems to me that, smitten with love for you and even quite mad, as though drunk in spirit, hiding the fact that her origins were in the highest divinity, he became a mortal man capable of suffering but without losing his divinity, and descending from the imperial court and kingdom, became a pilgrim and stranger, and like a poor beggar went in want through the world, as the gospel makes clear when it says that the crowd of priests said about him: "We do not know whence he comes" (Jo 9.19).

(17) So, think that so boundless has been the greatness of his perfect and incomprehensible love that he wished for you to be joined to him. Moreover, he descended from such a great height

in such a vile and wretched lowliness, undertaking such a tiring pilgrimage, just as the prophet Jeremiah testifies: "He dwelt among the peoples and found no rest" (Lam 1.3). I would have much to say about these pious and compassionate words were I to consider how the opposite is now found to be true of those persons who are named followers of Christ; but because that is not my task, I will keep quiet.

(18) I return to the theme of my nudity and see that I have not reflected the unbounded love of the most gentle lamb, Christ Jesus, who wished that for me his beautiful, virginal and resplendent face would be so struck and defiled. Since I have not been marked by and practiced in his disgrace, it follows that I am bare of the principal virtue which is most necessary to me. For this reason, my most beloved mothers and sisters, I pray you please entreat the divine clemency to deign to pardon me and fulfill what was promised: "If the adulteress comes to me, and I will not marry her . . . ." (cf. Jer 3.6–12). (19) But your prudence, dear and gentle sisters who are such that it does not seem that I will ever be transformed into one of you, take care somehow and in good time that, unlike me, you will not be received into the number of the adulteresses; instead, like faithful and true spouses, choose so that when the eternal and heavenly Ruler asks for you and wishes quietly to celebrate your nuptials – to introduce you to the glorious bedchamber of his triumphant glory, so that for eternity you will be joined to his divine and most chaste love – you will not be found unsuitable and without the adornments which befit you and are necessary for such a great virginal spouse. And, even though I have named them so many times above, nevertheless, because they delight me, I gladly repeat them so that you may remember them better.

(20) My sweetest sisters, I have said emphatically that the dowry which Christ Jesus wants from you is that you be vigorous in the

battle, that is, strong and constant combatants. By means of the virtue of patience which you exercise, you can add to the dowry the above mentioned qualities, that is, the unflagging desire to suffer evil for Christ and in everything to desire zealously to bear and sustain many tribulations, desires, anxieties, slanders, derision and painful death from any quarter whatever; because, through these and similar things, you will be certain of having with you the nuptial adornments, that is, the insignia of Christ Jesus, who, as you know, says to his beloved spouse, the cross of love: "You bear me as I have suffered through you, my spouse." And he also says: "Whoever wishes to come after me, the fount of life, ought to go by the narrow way" (Lk 13.24). (21) Now, then, beloved sisters, you have in your memories the salutary condition of your adornments so you can safely gaze upon the grand and magnificent emissary which will be sent to you from your spouse, and thus adorned, you can receive his invitation and rise to great heights. Then how greatly will be your happiness as you taste the fruit of the anguished sufferings and labours which you have born with true patience, persevering in the place to which God has called you! If you do this, you will not fall back into my confusion and falsehood which, as I said above, is this, that I have not delighted in carrying the cross as befitted me; and so I can say justly that before God and men I do not foresee anything but ruin and confusion.

(22) Notwithstanding all this, I recall what the prophet said, that is: "Even if I shall die, I will hope in your mercy" (cf. Job 13.15), for I do not wish to depart from that excellent virtue called hope which, speaking to me in its kindness, says that,

I really will be able to climb into heaven,
if in this world I do not have a place to lay my head,
and there I will find great pleasure,
if I have always suffered some evils here,

and I will be much honoured there
if here for Christ's sake among the others,
I will be despised and afflicted and troubled,
and that in paradise I will be content,
if here I have not what I choose to want,
and in the sight of my God I will sing sweetly,
if I sing humbly in choir,
and by him I will be made immortal and impassible,
if here I do not fear death and suffering for his sake,
and I will be made empress of his kingdom,
if here for his sake I am poor and mendicant,
and if I persevere in his most chaste and virginal love,
without doubt I will rejoice through his goodness
with him in eternity. Amen.

(23) The peace of Christ, sweet love, be always in your hearts, dear mothers and sisters, and in the hearts of all Christian people through whom and from whom may our true and one God in perfect Trinity and the incarnate Word be blessed and praised forever. Amen.

NOTES

INTRODUCTION

1. We are grateful to Isobel Burke of University College, Dublin, for sharing information with us.

2. In her edition of *Le sette armi spirituali* (Padova: Antenore, 1985) Foletti discusses the manuscript and printing history of *Le sette armi spirituali* (93–110) and the sources for Catherine's life (1–15). She also devotes considerable effort to identifying the families of Catherine's father (16–40). Serena Spanò, "Per uno studio su Caterina da Bologna." *Studi medievali*, ser. 3, vol. 12, no. 2 (1971) 713–759, surveys the ample archival materials available regarding Catherine and suggests lines of research.

The list of sources may be summarised as follows. When Catherine died in 1463, a circular letter was sent to other Poor Clare convents notifying them of her death and the existence of her book. Sisters made copies of the book before its first published edition in 1475. Sr. Illuminata Bembo wrote a first *vita* (ed. F. van Ortroy, "Une vie italienne de S. Caterine de Bologne,"*Acta Bollandiana* 41 [1923] 386–416), probably before her more influential *Specchio de illuminatione* (1469), which deals with the saint's birth, death, and events after the death of the saint. The second and third parts of the *Specchio* reproduce substantially the circular letter and first vita and constitute only one-sixth of the work. Bembo's work is much like the *Vitae Patrum* which were much read then. She provides static examples of virtue, not a chronological biography. Bembo's work had limited circulation in manuscript form before it was first printed in 1787. The biography of Catherine which had the greatest success in the fifteenth and sixteenth centuries is that of Sabadino degli Arienti which was inserted in *Gynevera de le clare donne* (1472). He mined Bembo's *Specchio*, but rearranged the contents chronologically. Annexed to the first printing of *The Seven Spiritual Weapons* was a biography in verse attributed to Pietro Azzoguidi, canon of S. Petronio. He is first to invoke Catherine as patronness of Bologna.

In 1502 appeared the first separately printed biography of the saint. It was written by Dionisio Paleotti, a Observant Friar Minor and confessor at Corpus Domini. He added four chapters on miracles. This remained the standard life for a century.

Catherine's work had its greatest popularity in the sixteenth century when there were seven editions of *Le sette armi spirituali* in Italian as well as a French and a Latin translation. The last significant contribution to Catherine's biography is that of Giovambattista Melloni, a follower of the Bollandists. His work is the most comprehensive and fundamental still today.

The following summary of Catherine's life, except where the notes indicate otherwise, is based on Maurizio Muccioli, OFM, *Santa Caterina da Bologna, Mistica del Quattrocento* (Bologna: Antoniano, 1963).

3. van Ortroy, 389, for texts about how these two siblings were helped by Catherine's prayers.

4. The Apostolic Clerics of St. Jerome were founded by Bl. John Colombini about 1360. They were called "Gesuati" because they liked to begin and end their sermons with the cry "Praised be Jesu" or "Hail Jesus." For the introduction of the new devotion to the Holy Name in England see Eamon Duffy, *The Stripping of the Altars* (New Haven: Yale, 1992) 45, 113–116, 236.

5. It seems Catherine penned other writings besides *Le sette armi spirituali.* There is, for example, a *Breviarium*, the artistic decoration of which is attributed to her. See Lucius Nuñez, "Descriptio Breviarii Manuscripti S. Catharinae Boniensis, o.s.cl.," *Archivum Franciscanum Historicum* 4 (1911) 732–747; Hans Vollmer, ed., Thieme-Becker, *Allgemeines Lexikon der Bildenden Künstler*, (Leipzig, Seemann) 34: 359. Isobel Burke

sent us a copy of Gilberto Sgarbi's edition of Catherine's *I Dodici Giardini* (Bologna: Sintesi, 1996), but we did not receive it in time to use it in this work. Sgarbi's edition of Catherine's short work is accompanied by a modern Italian translation and several prefaces on Catherine's life and mystical teaching. The work itself traces the stages of a person's growth toward mystical union with God.

6. *The Seven Spiritual Weapons*, VII (95–96).

7. *Ibid.*, VII (110).

8. *Ibid.*, IX (2), VII (110).

9. *Ibid.*, IX (2).

10. *Ibid.*, IX (2), VII (67), and perhaps X (4).

11. *Ibid.*, VII (8) + Preface (1). The events described in VII (69–70) and VII (98–99) do not seem to be autobiographical.

12. *Ibid.*, VII (38).

13. *Ibid.*, (100–102, 108).

14. *Ibid.*, VII (94).

15. Illuminata Bembo was the daughter of Lorenzo Bembo, a member of a wealthy Venetian family. She entered religious life in 1430. She was with Catherine from then until the latter's death. Sr. Illuminata was abbess at Corpus Domini in Bologna after Catherine. She died in 1493. Her *Specchio d'Illuminazione* is an important source for Catherine's life and character (see note 1). Muccioli relies on it heavily. See Muccioli, pp. 215–217.

16. Muccioli, 129. For other guidelines for prayer, see pp. 131, 153–157.

17. Muccioli, 158–162.

18. Cecilia Foletti, ed., *Le sette armi spirituali*, 165–177.

19. Elizabeth Alvilda Petroff, *Body and Soul: Essays on Medieval Women and Mysticism* (New York: Oxford, 1994) 110–130.

20. Petroff, 161–177.

21. See John Coakley, introduction to *Creative Women in Medieval and Early Modern Italy: A Religious and Aritistic Renaissance*, ed. E. Ann Matter and John Coakley (Philadelphia: University of Pennsylvania Press, 1994), 11, 13.

22. *The Seven Spiritual Weapons*, VII (10), VII (15), VII (28).
23. *Ibid.*, VII (37).
24. *Ibid.*, VII (110).
25. *Ibid.*, X (1,3).
26. *Ibid.*, VII (30–33).
27. *Ibid.*, VII (34–36).
28. *The Seven Spiritual Weapons*, X (15).
29. *Ibid.*, X (1–2).
30. In this section, written by Marilyn Hall, it seemed better to include the chapter and paragraph numbers in the text.

31. *The Diagnostic and Statistical Manual of Mental Disorders* (Washington, DC: American Psychiatric Association) 320, 327.

THE SEVEN SPIRITUAL WEAPONS

32. John 8.12. Biblical and liturgical quotations are in Latin in the original text. Catherine occasionally quotes from other sources, especially Jacopone da Todi. All our translations are based on the quotations as they appear in Foletti's text.

33. The antecedent of this seems to be "to do whatever good you can." A century later the Council of Trent spoke of the same situation: Session 6, Decr. de Justificatione, c. 14 (DS #1542–#1544).

34. Jacopone da Todi, *Laude* 78, vv. 132–134. Foletti numbers the *Laude* according to the edition of F. Mancini (Rome–Bari, 1974). This differs from the more traditional numbering used by Serge and Elizabeth Hughes in their American translation (New York: Paulist, 1982).

35. Migne, *Patrologia Latina* 73: 911–912.

36. The modern Italian "manna" has the more general meaning of "blessing."

37. St. Francis, *Admonitions* 3.

38. Roman Breviary, Antiphon for Vespers, November 22.

39. Here and below "colpa" (literally, "fault") seems to refer to the practice of "culpa," a regular disclosure of faults against the rule of their community which religious made to their superiors or at a community meeting. See the article A. Gauthier, art. "Colpa," in *Dizionario degli istituti di perfezione* (1975) 2:1237–1239.

40. See previous note.

41. Jacopone da Todi, *Laude* 92, vv. 341–344.

42. St. Bernard, Sermon 2 on the Solemnity of the Apostles Peter and Paul, *Opera*, ed. J. Leclercq and H. Rochais (Rome: 1968) 5: 190.6; also, *The Sayings of Brother Egidius* (*Detti di Frate Egidio in Mistici del Duecento e del Trecento*, ed. A. Levasti [Milano, 1960] 131).

43. Palladius, *Historia lausiaca*, ed. W. K. Lowther Clarke (London, 1918) 22 (*Patrologia Latina* 73: 1126).

44. Jacobus de Voragine, *The Golden Legend*, tr. Granger Ryan and Helmut Ripperger (New York: Longmans, Green, 1941) 317-318 (June 18) and 539–543 (September 11).

45. *Detti de Frate Egidio*, 123.

46. St. Bernard, Sermon 5 on the Festival of All Saints, 9, ed. Leclercq, 5: 8–10.

47. *Detti di Frate Egidio*, 128.

48. Here and in IX.14 "*fraternidade*" is translated "sisterhood".

49. This paragraph, partly in Italian and partly in Latin, is not easy to interpret: "Ma chi de zò ne ssia caxone, saperasse nello rendere delli debiti, conzosiacossa che li soprastanti alcune volte, inganati *sub nomine et vochabulo sensualitatis si impendunt altissime caritatis*, ponendo innanci a le greze loro quello che per sí non poria rodere né smaltire."

BIBLIOGRAPHY

Gordini, Gian Domenico. "Caterina da Bologna," *Biblioteca sanctorum* 3: 980–982.

Heerinckx, Jacques. "Catherine de Bologne (Sainte)," *Dictionnaire de spiritualité* 2: 288–290.

Matter, E. Ann, and John Coakley. Eds. *Creative Women in Medieval and Early Modern Italy: A Religious and Artistic Renaissance.* Philadelphia: University of Pennsylvania Press, 1994.

Muccioli, Maurizio, OFM. *Santa Caterina da Bologna, Mistica del Quattrocento.* Bologna: Antoniano, 1963.

Nuñez, Lucius. "Descriptio breviarii manuscripti S. Catharinae Bononiensis, O.S.CL.," *Archivum franciscanum historicum* 4 (1911), 732–747.

Ortroy, F. van. "Une vie italienne de Sainte Catherine de Bologne," *Analecta bollandiana* 41 (1923), 386–416.

Petroff, Elizabeth Alvida. Ed. *Body and Soul: Essays on Medieval Women and Mysticism.* New York: Oxford, 1994.

Spanò, Serena. "Per uno studio su Caterina da Bologna," *Studi medievali,* ser. 3, vol. 12, no. 2 (1971), 713–759.

Terpstra, Nicholas. "Confraternities and Mendicant Orders: The Dynamics of Lay and Clerical Brotherhood in Renaissance Bologna," *Catholic Historical Review* 82 (1996) 1–22.

Vegri [Vigri], Santa Caterina. *Le sette armi spirituali.* Ed. Cecilia Foletti. Medioevo e Umanesimo, 56. Padova: Editrice Antenore, 1985.

—. *I Dodici Giardini.* Ed. Gilberto Sgarbi. Bologna: Sintesi, 1996.

"Vigri (Vegri), Caterina." In *Allgemeines Lexikon der bildenden Künstler.* Ed. Hans Vollmer. Leipzig: Seemann. 34: 359.